Feeling Buddies

Self-Regulation Curriculum

by Dr. Becky A. Bailey
& Lety Valero

407.366.0233
648 Trestle Point, Sanford FL 32771
ConsciousDiscipline.com

Second Edition
© 2021 by Becky A. Bailey, Ph.D.
All rights reserved. Published by Loving Guidance, LLC.
Printed in the U.S.A.

Editor: Julie Ruffo
Cover / Page Design: Brandi Besher

Table of
Contents

Meet the Authors

Dr. Becky A. Bailey, Ph.D.

Dr. Becky Bailey is an award-winning author, renowned educator and internationally recognized expert in childhood education and developmental psychology. She is the creator of Conscious Discipline which has impacted an estimated 20 million children while inspiring and training more than 3.5 million educators and caregivers.

Conscious Discipline creates a compassionate culture and facilitates an intentional shift in adults' understanding of behavior via the Conscious Discipline Brain State Model. It then provides specific brain-friendly, research-backed strategies for responding to each child's individual needs with wisdom. This highly effective approach is proven to increase self-regulation, sense of safety, connection, empathy and intrinsic motivation in both children and adults. Conscious Discipline is practiced in over 73 countries with resource materials offered in 22 languages.

Over 2.5 million of Dr. Becky's fifteen top-selling book titles are in circulation and she is the recipient of over 30 product and program awards. She is the founder of Loving Guidance, Inc., dedicated to creating positive environments for children, families and schools. With over 35 years of experience working with the most difficult children, Dr. Bailey deeply believes we must transform the lives of adults first and children second.

Lety Valero, M.Ed.

Lety Valero has worked in education for over 20 years in bilingual settings, is a Conscious Discipline Master Instructor, has guided Eton School in school-wide implementation of Conscious Discipline and co-created the Feeling Buddies program with Dr. Becky Bailey.

She received her Masters in International Education from Endicott College in Boston.

Getting Started
with the Feeling Buddies Curriculum

Welcome to your *Feeling Buddies Curriculum.* You are about to embark on a very exciting journey! This *Curriculum* will guide you through the self-regulation process in the classroom, empowering you to help children be successful with this crucial life skill. You will use the *Curriculum* to teach basic self-regulation skills and coach children to use these skills with their Feeling Buddies. As the children help their Buddies handle tough emotions, they strengthen self-regulation skills within themselves. As you coach children in the process, you strengthen your own self-regulation skills. Both you and the children emerge from the experience with a wealth of healing and self-regulatory skills. What could be better than that?

The *Curriculum* contains seven units. The first six units contain five lessons each. The first unit is an introduction. The next five units address the five steps for self-regulation, with one step per unit. The final unit (Unit 7) contains a single closing lesson. The *Curriculum* builds in a progressive order to deepen our understanding of emotions and how to handle them. Children begin by learning to read body language and facial expressions in order to understand their emotions and label the feeling. Then they learn calming strategies so they can begin to put a pause between the emotion and an action. Ultimately, they learn problem-solving skills for handling the problem now and helping to prevent similar problems in the future. All conflict starts with upset. Without being able to regulate the upset, conflict resolution is impossible.

There's so much stuff! Where do I begin?

The *Feeling Buddies Self-Regulation Toolkit* is a comprehensive approach to teaching self-regulation. It is essential to familiarize yourself with all the materials in the *Toolkit*. Exploring every item will help you understand and teach self-regulation in a more effective manner.

The first step is to read *Managing Emotional Mayhem*. This book creates the foundation for the *Curriculum* to build on. *Mayhem* will help you understand the importance and significance of the skills you will teach and familiarizes you with the concepts in the *Curriculum*. It takes you on a journey of emotional self-discovery first and then empowers you with the skills needed to help children develop healthy emotional coping strategies. It coaches you to apply the skills of self-regulation in your personal life, giving you a deeper, more personal understanding of what you are about to teach. Finally, it steps you through the skills you need to help children with the process as you apply the *Curriculum*. **It is essential you read the book before you begin using the *Curriculum* in your classroom.**

Buddy Tip: Organizing a book study group with peers is a wonderful forum for bouncing ideas off each other, sharing "aha" moments and adding enjoyment to the learning process as you implement the *Curriculum*.

Watch Dr. Bailey and Conscious Discipline Master Instructor Amy Speidel on ConsciousDiscipline.com. Watch Dr. Bailey and Master Instructor Amy Speidel's Conscious Comedy Skits on (consciousdiscipline.com/comedy). This series of videos uses humor to explore our relationship with our emotions. Watching the videos will also help you complete the evaluation on page 62 in *Managing Emotional Mayhem*.

Watch the instructional DVD to see the *Toolkit* in action with real children as you read *Managing Emotional Mayhem* (ideally during Chapter 3 or later). The DVD brings the scenarios in the book and *Curriculum* to life, helping you better understand how to coach children when conflict and upset arise and the importance of your role in the process. You will observe real teachers and children encountering teachable moments and utilizing the Safe Place. You will also see how to use the songs in the lessons, whether they include clapping games, contain specific movements or require actions with the Feeling Buddies.

Become familiar with the songs on the *Listen to Your Feelings* CD. Be sure to listen to the songs needed for each lesson a few times before starting. This will help you become familiar with the tunes and lyrics so you can clearly identify the message each song teaches.

Spend some time with your Buddies. Look at each Feeling Buddy carefully to understand its message to you. Look at its eyes, eyebrows and mouth. Become friends with the Buddies as you read *Managing Emotional Mayhem*. Notice when they are with you in your daily life. Notice when you accept them and when you reject them. Which Buddies have you established healthy relationships with and which ones are you in unhealthy relationships with? How do these relationships change as you read and implement the concepts in *Managing Emotional Mayhem*?

Ready, click, go! Your *Toolkit* includes a CD-Rom full of helpful resources and blackline master reproducibles in Mac and PC-friendly PDF form. Some *Curriculum* lessons require reproducible worksheets or templates. Other lessons include optional extension activities that use reproducibles. Read the lessons, decide which reproducibles you will use and then print as many of them as you need. These reproducibles are an aid for increasing the connection and learning that children experience with each lesson. If you teach Pre-K or Kindergarten please use the reproducibles sparingly. It is the belief of Conscious Discipline that young children learn best through experience, and the *Curriculum* is designed to give children many opportunities to interact with the Feeling Buddies and each other.

Familiarize yourself with additional tools. Some of the lessons include additional tools for learning. Some of these items, like the Shubert books, are included. Some of these items, like the chart paper and markers, are not included. Make sure you compile the necessary items and know the purpose of each item before conducting each lesson. For example, before reading a Shubert book to the children, read it yourself to understand its purpose and message within the lesson.

Set up your Safe Place. You will coach children in using the Safe Place with the five-step self-regulation process over the course of Units 2 to 6. Prepare this learning center for use before you begin the *Curriculum*. Model it after the labeled image on page xiv and the information in Chapter 5 of *Managing Emotional Mayhem*. Watch the video "Setting Up Your Safe Place" on your DVD. You might choose to keep this learning center taped off as "closed" until Lesson 2.4, which includes a ribbon-cutting ceremony. If you choose to open the Safe Place before Lesson 2.4, wait to place the Feeling Buddies and posters until after the lesson. Resources for setting up your Safe Place include:

- Page xiv in this *Curriculum*
- *Managing Emotional Mayhem*, Chapter 5
- *Creating the School Family*, Chapter 9
- The Safe Place in Shubert's classroom: ConsciousDiscipline.com/Shubert
- *Shubert is a S.T.A.R.*

Will teaching the Curriculum be enough?

The effectiveness of the *Toolkit* is predicated on the use of three teaching methods used together:

1. Daily teachable moments,
2. The Safe Place Self-Regulation Learning Center and
3. The songs and activities in the *Feeling Buddies Curriculum*.

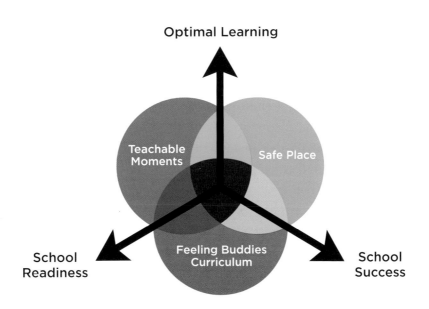

All three components are essential to learning. Success requires information about how to do something, coaching as the situation arises in daily contexts and the opportunity to accomplish the task by ourselves. None of these teaching methods can be truly successful alone! The teachable moments give you the opportunity to reinforce the concepts from the *Curriculum* lessons in context, and the Safe Place is where children go to practice the skills you are teaching.

Children often feel sad when a friend moves to another school or angry when someone grabs a toy. They feel disappointed at not being able to share something that was important to them or not getting something they really wanted. It can be frustrating trying to complete a puzzle or write a complex paragraph. Emotional situations happen often in the context of school. They serve as valuable ways to reinforce the *Curriculum* lessons through teachable moments and Safe Place use, so don't miss the chance to use them as learning opportunities.

How long will it take to teach the Curriculum lessons?

The lessons will take about 20 minutes each, with an average of two lessons per week. The *Curriculum* provides you with the flexibility to choose how often to teach the lessons. You may find that your students grasp a concept quickly and choose to do three lessons that week. You may encounter a lesson that requires greater effort from your students. In this case, you would only undertake one lesson and practice it all week. It will be helpful to spend additional time on a lesson any time enthusiasm is high or understanding is low. You may also decide that conducting all five lessons in a unit is not necessary. You may want to try and cover the *Curriculum* in the first 18 weeks so children can begin using the Feeling Buddies in the Safe Place and learn how to move through the five-step process of self-regulation. As the year progresses, go back, reteach and add extension activities to deepen understanding.

As you implement the lessons, you will realize how important it is for children to share their personal experiences. However, due to time restraints you may wish to do the following:

1. Limit the number of children who share;
2. Use "Turn and Talk" sticks with younger children and/or encourage older students to share with a partner. (A pair of Turn and Talk sticks consists of two tongue depressors, one with a mouth cutout glued to it to designate the speaker and one with an ear cutout glued to it to designate the listener.)
3. Use a small group format to teach the lesson.

The drawback to lessening sharing in order to save time is this: Children, especially children in the four-to-six year age range, have a developmental need to share their life experience with adults. Limiting sharing limits adult contact. Turn and talk sticks structure partner sharing for young students, but do not provide the kind of adult validation that fosters optimal development. As you plan your lessons, be certain to balance partner sharing and other share-limiting strategies with ample time for children to share with adults.

Should I follow the lessons word for word?

The *Curriculum* is a teaching guide that contains helpful words, activities and examples. You know your group of children well enough to understand what will work as it is written and what might need to be adjusted. Allow each lesson to spark your own creativity and brilliance!

The *Curriculum* also contains blackline master reproducibles. While these pencil and paper activities are helpful for practicing the information discussed in the *Curriculum*, they are not the core of the program. This *Curriculum* is a living, breathing, interactive and engaging process built on a foundation of connection, music, movement and dynamic classroom life. Do not let the optional paper-and-pencil activities replace that connection.

As you proceed through the lessons, remember connection is at the heart of this *Curriculum*. Your goal is to process the *Curriculum* information so it becomes second nature; you can adapt it to the needs of your children and you can be present to connect with them. Use the *Curriculum* as a guide, not a map.

What if I have a large group?

The program is proven to work in small or large groups. You may have 22 children and one adult in a class, and still enjoy great success with this *Curriculum*. With any size group, you will need to budget your time so lessons flow in the designated timeframe. If your structure allows it, you may wish to work with half of your group while the other half works on something else and then switch tasks. You may also wish to use the paired sharing discussed in "How long will it take to teach the *Curriculum* lessons?" to give everyone the opportunity to share, even in the largest groups. Again, it is important to understand that children ages four through six need to share experiences with a responsive, caring adult. "Pair and share with a friend" techniques are more developmentally appropriate for First Grade and older. At any age, it is essential to balance pair-and-share strategies with time to share with adults.

How do I check for understanding?

You will start seeing results soon after you start implementing the *Curriculum*. The children grasp these concepts and apply them to everyday life situations rapidly. The teachable moments that arise in your class will be one of the most effective ways to assess the acquisition of knowledge. Another way is to look for the following behaviors.

The child is able to:

- ❑ Give a name to the emotion, identifying feelings in everyday situations.
- ❑ Identify feelings in others by observing their faces and act in helpful ways in response to others' emotions.
- ❑ Put a pause between the feeling and the response to it. (This is made visible with healthy responses.)
- ❑ Become aware of triggers, verbalize them and plan ahead to handle them in helpful ways.
- ❑ Practice breathing techniques (S.T.A.R., Drain, Balloon, Pretzel) in an upset state to regain composure.
- ❑ Offer empathy to others when upset and suggest the Safe Place as a way to regain composure.
- ❑ Go to the Safe Place when intense emotions bubble up.
- ❑ Identify the emotion and choose the corresponding Feeling Buddy.
- ❑ Use calming and choice items in the Safe Place purposefully.
- ❑ Follow the self-regulation process in the Safe Place (when coached by the teacher).
- ❑ Follow the self-regulation process in the Safe Place (when alone).
- ❑ Describe where he/she feels the feeling in his/her body.
- ❑ Choose healthy ways to respond to the message embedded in basic feelings:
    - ❑ Seeks comfort when sad
    - ❑ Asks for help when scared
    - ❑ Calms and changes when angry

Additional assessment tools are located on page xvi of the *Curriculum*.
1. Rubrics and teacher evaluations
2. Self-evaluations for children

What else will help me be successful as I teach this Curriculum?

The *Feeling Buddies Curriculum* is based on a bigger program called Conscious Discipline. Learning more about creating the School Family and the Seven Powers and Seven Basic Skills of Conscious Discipline is a valuable tool when implementing this *Curriculum*. There is a wealth of information about Conscious Discipline online at ConsciousDiscipline.com, where you will find Shubert's school, webinars and other free resources. The Conscious Discipline Facebook page provides a wonderful forum for information sharing: Facebook.com/ConsciousDiscipline. There is a YouTube channel at YouTube.com/LovingGuidance that contains helpful videos. And, of course, there is no substitution for the life-changing experience of attending an official Conscious Discipline event like the Summer Institute (CD1) or one of our many nationwide workshops. At the end of each unit, a section titled "Additional Resources" will guide you to specific Conscious Discipline items that are helpful for that unit.

Have Fun!

This *Curriculum* will change your relationship with your emotions, promote emotional well-being and improve all of your significant relationships. Guaranteed!

Managing the Program

Green Text
Spoken words
from the Buddies

Black Text
Directions and
explanations for teacher

Blue Text
Spoken words of
the teacher

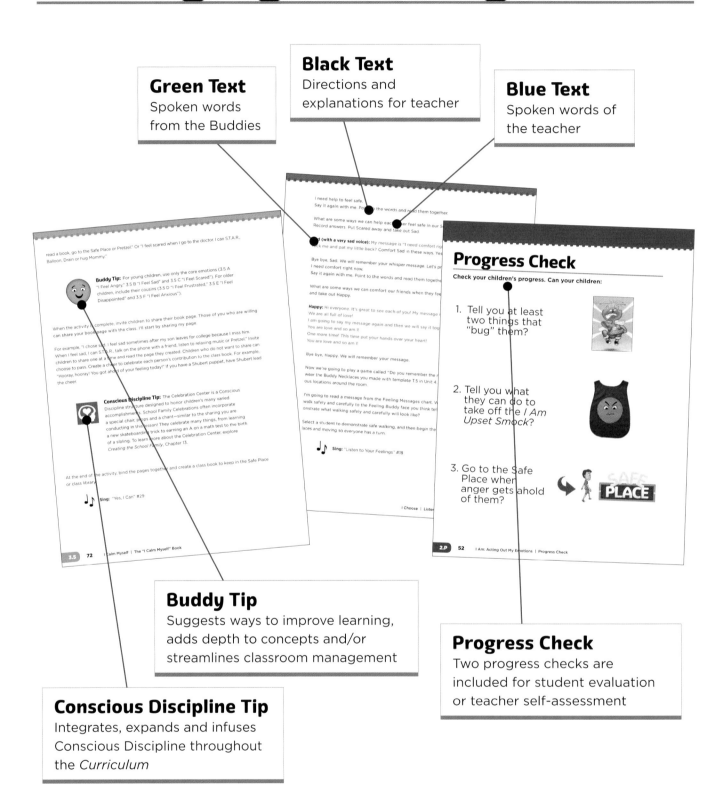

Buddy Tip
Suggests ways to improve learning,
adds depth to concepts and/or
streamlines classroom management

Conscious Discipline Tip
Integrates, expands and infuses
Conscious Discipline throughout
the *Curriculum*

Progress Check
Two progress checks are
included for student evaluation
or teacher self-assessment

Extensions
Optional activities enrich the learning experience, integrate home and school, and/or extend the lesson

Resources
Additional Conscious Discipline products and resources

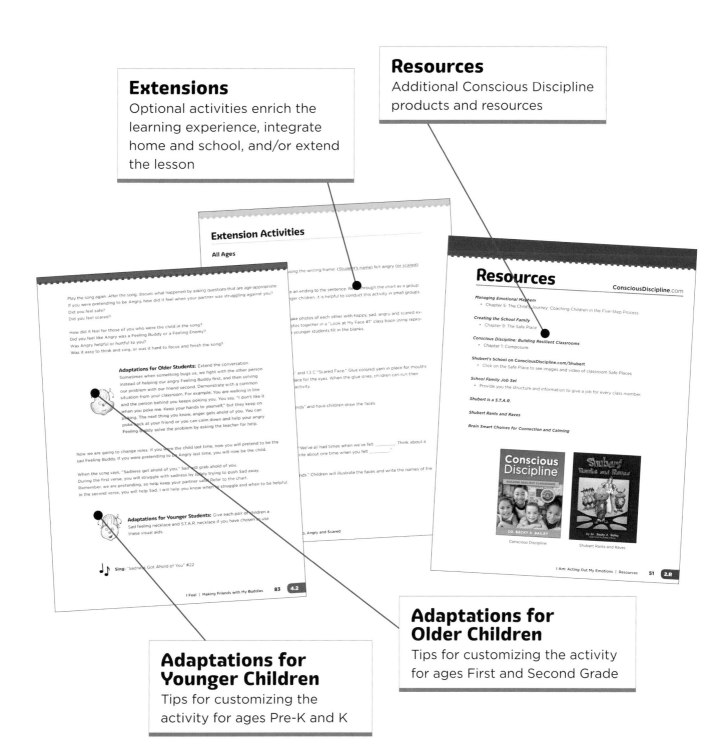

Adaptations for Younger Children
Tips for customizing the activity for ages Pre-K and K

Adaptations for Older Children
Tips for customizing the activity for ages First and Second Grade

Model Safe Place

I Calm Poster
Provides children with visual icons of the four basic calming strategies.

My Five Steps Chart
Provides visuals for teachers and children to conduct the five steps to self-regulation.

Safe Place Case
A container to hold all the items listed on the I Choose to Think poster, plus other items to help children organize and calm, including but not limited to the *Helping My Feeling Buddies* book (the *I Can Calm* and *When I Feel* books are helpful options available at ConsciousDiscipline.com).

Brain Smart® Choices for Connection and Calming
Provide an additional 20 connecting activities and 16 calming activities for your Safe Place. The *Choice Cubes* are optional.

Caring Connections Poster

Provides four options for children who feel upset and want additional connection to help them turn on their thinking brains.

I Choose to Think Poster

Provides six basic choices to help children turn on their thinking brains after an upsetting event.

Feeling Buddies and Their Pocket Home

The heart of the program. Children select the Feeling Buddy that matches their emotional state. As they help their Buddy regulate, they learn how to regulate themselves.

Bean Bag or Soft Cushions

Creates a comfortable and inviting space for children to relax while implementing the five-step process of self-regulation.

Safe Place Mat

A textured mat displaying the four basic calming strategies. The mat is optional.

I Am Upset Smock

Integral to teaching and modeling when and why to go to the Safe Place.

Assessments

Rating Criteria

1 = **Not Yet.** There is no evidence the child has grasped the concept. The desired behavior is not seen when a situation arises in context. The child needs to be encouraged and coached to achieve the desired behavior.

2 = **Occasionally.** There is at least one occasion in which the desired behavior was evident. The skill is still developing. The child needs encouragement and coaching to display the behavior in multiple contexts.

3 = **Evident.** The child has demonstrated on multiple occasions that the desired behavior has become a pattern. The child demonstrates the desired behavior independently, with no encouragement or coaching.

🅘 Am | Emotional Awareness

Children develop awareness of their own feelings and of those with whom they interact. Concepts woven throughout *Curriculum*; most evident in Units 1 and 2.

	1	2	3
1. Recognizes and names their feelings in everyday situations			
2. Recognizes and names the feelings of others			
3. Draws feeling faces that represent the core feelings			
4. Names all Feeling Buddies			
5. Is aware feelings can give off face, body and voice signals			
6. Is aware feelings produce sensations in the body			
7. Identifies emotional triggers			
8. Understands the link between emotional triggers and behaviors			
9. Takes themselves to the Safe Place when needed			

	1	2	3

ⓘ Calm | Emotional Regulation

Children learn to put a pause between impulse and response. Concepts woven throughout *Curriculum*; most evident in Unit 3.

	1	2	3
10. Calms themselves with adult assistance			
11. Performs the S.T.A.R., Drain, Balloon and Pretzel			
12. Goes to the Safe Place and purposely selects a calming activity			
13. Demonstrates belly breathing			
14. Verbalizes triggers and plans how to handle them in helpful ways			

ⓘ Feel | Regulatory Self-talk

Children develop the foundation of empathy toward others and healthy use of regulatory self-talk with the Feeling Buddies. Concepts woven throughout *Curriculum*; most evident in Unit 4.

	1	2	3
15. Selects the Feeling Buddy that best represents their feeling state			
16. Accepts the feeling by greeting and welcoming it *(Hello Anger. Welcome Anger.)*			
17. Names the feeling for the Feeling Buddy *(You seem angry.)*			
18. Helps the Feeling Buddy calm *(Breathe with me. Holds and strokes the Buddy on its back.)*			
19. Encourages the Feeling Buddy *(You can handle this.)*			

ⓘ Choose | Focused Attention

Children begin engaging their brains, focusing their attention and preparing to re-enter class activities ready to learn. Concepts woven throughout *Curriculum*; most evident in Unit 5.

	1	2	3
20. Chooses from a list of options or presents choices after an emotional upset			
21. Able to focus attention after emotional upset			

ⓘ Solve | Conflict Resolution

Children are empowered to be helpful instead of hurtful in social interactions as well as follow the rules of the classroom. Concepts woven throughout *Curriculum*; most evident in Unit 6.

	1	2	3
22. Puts a pause between impulse and action, and chooses healthy positive responses to daily conflicts			
23. Follows the five-step self-regulation process in the Safe Place with assistance			
24. Follows the five-step self-regulation process in the Safe Place independently			
25. Sees problems differently and returns to class to address the original trigger with new skills			

Notes:

_____

_____

_____

_____

_____

_____

_____

_____

_____

_____

_____

_____

_____

_____

_____

Additional Social-Emotional Skills Assessment

As children learn the comprehensive skill of self-regulation, the following social skills will become more visible in the classroom.

Helpfulness

	1	2	3
1. Is helpful to others with words and actions			
2. Is helpful to the teacher with words and actions			

Social Skills

	1	2	3
3. Assertively stands up for self by saying, "I don't like it when ___. Please ___."			
4. Asks the teacher for help when unfairly treated			
5. Assists other children in calming down or going to the Safe Place to help keep the classroom safe			
6. Knows how to share, ask for a turn, wait for a turn, manage personal space and handle classroom transitions			
7. Uses available language skills (verbal, nonverbal, signing) to get needs met, with adult assistance			
8. Accepts guidance and direction			
9. Plays safely with others and can lead or follow in play situations			
10. Follows directions and persists with tasks with assistance			

Empathy

	1	2	3
11. Notices peers' distress and offers helpfulness			
12. Assists others in calming down and managing emotions			
13. Suggests others use the Safe Place in the classroom when needed			
14. Assists others with conflict resolution strategies			
15. Sees from other person's perspective with assistance			

Alignments

Feeling Buddies Unit + Skill Descriptions	NAEYC Standards	CSEFEL Inventory of Practices
Unit 1: Meet the Buddies Emotional Awareness: Children develop awareness of their own feelings and the feelings of those with whom they interact **Unit 2: I Am: Acting Out My Emotions** Emotional Awareness: Children develop awareness of their own feelings and of those with whom they interact **Unit 3: I Calm Myself** Emotional Regulation: Children learn to put a pause between impulse and response **Unit 4: I Feel** Regulatory Self-Talk: Children develop the foundation of empathy toward others and self-regulation when using self-talk with the Feeling Buddies **Unit 5: I Choose** Focused Attention: Children begin engaging their brains, focusing their attention and preparing to re-enter class activities ready to continue learning **Unit 6: I Solve** Conflict Resolution: Children are empowered to be helpful instead of hurtful in social interactions and follow the rules of the classroom	• 1.A: Building Positive Relationships Among Teachers and Families • 1.B: Building Positive Relationships Between Teachers and Children • 1.C: Helping Children Make Friends • 1.D: Creating a Predictable, Consistent, and Harmonious Classroom • 1.E: Addressing Challenging Behaviors • 1.F: Promoting Self-Regulation • 2.B: Areas of Development: Social-Emotional Development	• Develops meaningful relationship with children and families • Examines personal, family and cultural views of child's challenging behavior • Examines own attitudes toward challenging behavior • Ensures smooth transitions • Designs activities to promote engagement • Uses positive feedback and encouragement • Interacts with children to develop their self-esteem • Encourages Autonomy • Capitalizes on the presence of typically developing peers • Uses prompting and reinforcement of interactions effectively • Provides instructional in the development of social skills • Promotes identification and labeling of emotions in self and others • Explores the nature of feelings and the appropriate ways they can be expressed • Models appropriate expressions and labeling of their own emotions and self-regulation throughout the course of the day • Creates a planned approach for problem-solving processes within the classroom • Promotes children's individualized emotional regulation that will enhance positive social interactions within the classroom • Teams use functional assessment • Teaches replacement skills • Monitors progress

Head Start Early Learning Outcomes Framework

DOMAIN: Approaches to Learning
- Emotional and Behavioral Self-Regulation
- Cognitive Self-Regulation (Executive Functioning)
- Initiative and Curiosity
- Creativity

DOMAIN: Social and Emotional Development
- Relationships with Adults
- Relationships with Other Children
- Emotional Functioning
- Sense of Identity and Belonging

DOMAIN: Language and Literacy
- Attending and Understanding
- Communicating and Speaking
- Vocabulary

DOMAIN: Cognition
- Exploration and Discovery
- Memory
- Imitation and Symbolic Representation and Play

DOMAIN: Perceptual, Motor, and Physical Development
- Perception
- Health, Safety, and Nutrition

Student Self-Assessment

1. I can name two things that bug me.
   - ❏ Yes
   - ❏ No

2. When a feeling gets ahold of me, I go to the Safe Place.
   - ❏ Yes
   - ❏ No

3. I know how to take off the *I Am Upset Smock*.
   - ❏ Yes
   - ❏ No

4. I know how to calm down in the Safe Place.
   - ❏ Yes
   - ❏ No

5. I can pick a Feeling Buddy that shows how I feel.

❏ Yes

❏ No

6. I can keep my Feeling Buddy safe.

❏ Yes

❏ No

7. I can choose to turn my thinking brain on.

❏ Yes

❏ No

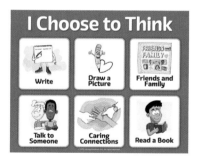

8. I can find solutions to my problems after I have calmed down.

❏ Yes

❏ No

Challenging Children

Help for Teachers

Each day, in every classroom, there are thousands of human-to-human interactions. Teachers and children communicate with words, smiles and open arms. Each day, in every classroom, there are also thousands of aggressive and non-compliant acts. Disconnected children act out their pain on teachers and other children.

Early childhood teachers realize the importance of connecting with and fostering social competence in young children, yet they often feel so overwhelmed by disruptive behavior that they resort to traditional negative forms of discipline, like yelling, time out, punishment, tangible rewards and reduced playtime. These responses may yield short-term relief, but they do not bring about long-term changes.

There is hope! Embedding the *Feeling Buddies Curriculum* within a Conscious Discipline School Family is an effective solution, especially for children with persistently challenging behaviors.

Administrators and Response to Intervention (RTI)

Response to Intervention (RTI) uses a tiered intervention model to address the needs of children. The three tiers indicate the level of intensity or type of intervention necessary to address a child's learning or behavioral problems.

Tier 1 consists of universal, school-wide interventions that meet the needs of most children. About 80 to 85 percent of children will learn the social-emotional skills needed for school success using an effective classroom management program.

It is imperative that Administrators:

1. Implement Conscious Discipline school or agency-wide. Contact Conscious Discipline to begin your journey now.
2. Implement the *Feeling Buddies Self-Regulation Toolkit*.

Tier 2 represents about 5 to 10 percent of the children who will need additional resources to learn to manage their behavior, control their emotional outburst and focus their attention.

It is imperative that Administrators:

1. Provide small group opportunities to coach young children in Conscious Discipline skills, structures, routines and rituals.
2. Provide small group opportunities to coach children through the five-step self-regulation process in the Safe Place.

Tier 3 represents about 1 to 5 percent of children. These children require the most intense interventions for successful outcome. Tier 3 requires one-on-one coaching and intervention.

It is imperative that Administrators:

1. Provide ongoing training in Conscious Discipline for a key staff person. This person will be responsible for your Conscious Discipline RTI program, with a focus on the Tier 3 children.
2. Designate a Safe Place coach. One person at the school will be your self-regulation expert.

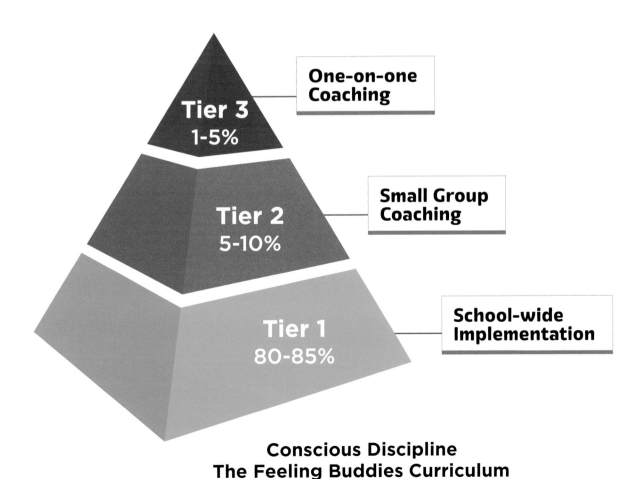

**Conscious Discipline
The Feeling Buddies Curriculum**

An Administrator's Perspective by Lety Valero

As a principal, I decided to create a Safe Place in my office for several reasons. First, we are all in this together. If I expected the teachers to create a Safe Place, I thought it would be important to set the example. I made my office Safe Place as complete and as engaging as possible, so as to help inspire my teachers. It would serve as a model for everyone in the campus. Second, for me to coach and help teachers in using the Safe Place appropriately, I needed to use it and practice it as well. Third, our school needed a place where the most challenging children could receive the self-regulation assistance they needed. My Safe Place provided that in a more private, more intensely-focused setting.

Ari's Success Story

Ari entered our school a year and a half ago. Ari's teacher had created a cozy Safe Place containing the items in the *Feeling Buddies Toolkit*, a variety of additional relaxation tools in a Safe Place Case and box of family photo albums parents made during back-to-school night. As the school year progressed, other children used the Safe Place as they needed it and began successfully

self-regulating. It was different with Ari. When he was upset, he would immediately lose control and go to the Safe Place, only to wreak havoc. He threw everything in the Safe Place Case, tore up the feeling books and destroyed family albums.

The Safe Place wasn't working for Ari! His teacher and I did some observation and problem solving. We decided Ari needed some one-on-one coaching out of the classroom on how to conduct the five-step process. When an upset would happen, he would come to my office or I would go get him and join him in my office Safe Place. I would coach him to breathe and relax. It wasn't easy! He would run away halfway through the process, resist relaxing and battle against my efforts to coach him.

About six months passed. Ari gave us many opportunities to practice our own composure skills, and ultimately we began to wonder if this structure that worked wonders for the rest of our students simply wouldn't work for this particular child. We chose to see his behavior as a call for help, and never gave up on him. We continued to coach him one-on-one in the Safe Place.

One day, another upset child went to the Safe Place. Ari began to coach her. He reminded her to breathe and took deep breaths with her. He helped her choose the Buddy that showed how she felt. He encouraged her to pick cranky cream to relax herself. He reminded her it was okay to feel sad. Finally, he suggested she take the Sad Buddy back to her seat with her.

Ari had been learning to use the Safe Place all those months! He still has a very difficult time managing his emotions and gets easily triggered, but a year later, he is independently taking himself to the Safe Place and following the five-step self-regulation process. He has become committed to helping others in the process and coaches his friends in the Safe Place. He even suggests solutions to the problems that initiate their upsets!

Meet the Buddies

Hello, Happy and Sad

Goal: To identify and name facial cues for the emotional states of happy and sad

Materials

- [ ] *Listen to Your Feelings* CD Songs:
  - "It's Buddy Time" #16
  - "Look at My Face Part 1" #19
  - "Bye, Bye Buddies" #4
- [ ] Happy and Sad Feeling Buddies
- [ ] Reproducibles
  - 1.1 A, 1.1 B (optional, younger)
- [ ] Empty Feeling Buddies pocket board
- [ ] Chart paper or sentence strips
- [ ] Instructional DVD
- [ ] *Managing Emotional Mayhem*
- [ ] Turn and Talk sticks (optional)
- [ ] Talking stick (optional)
- [ ] Happy/Sad sticks (optional, younger)
- [ ] Yarn, googly eyes, crayons (optional, younger)

Word Wall

Happy, Sad

Before You Begin

- Watch "Overview by Dr. Becky Bailey" and the first two videos in the "Circle Time" section ("Overview of the Curriculum" and "Overview of the Songs") on your instructional DVD
- Watch the songs for Lesson 1.1 by selecting "Circle Time" then "Songs By Lesson" on your instructional DVD
- Review *Managing Emotional Mayhem*, Chapter 3
- Listen to "Look at My Face Part 1"
- Gather materials
- Write Happy and Sad's chants on chart paper or sentence strips
- Write the words to "Look at My Face Part 1" on chart paper, leaving the feeling word blank. Laminate the chart paper. Write the feeling words as you say them during the lesson. (optional)
- Make Turn and Talk sticks (optional)
- Make Happy/Sad sticks (optional, younger)
- **Word Wall:** Happy, Sad

Let's Get Started

 Sing: "It's Buddy Time" #16

Keep the Feeling Buddies hidden behind your back, under a blanket or in a basket until you introduce them.

I have really been looking forward to our lesson today! I am going to introduce some new friends to you. They are our Feeling Buddies and they will be very helpful in our classroom. Before I introduce them to you, I have a question for you. Have you ever felt happy?

We've all had times when we feel happy. This is one of our new friends, Happy. Hold up the happy Feeling Buddy. **One time I felt happy when...** Share a personal story. Hold Happy next to your face as you share your story.

Buddy Tip: When sharing stories with children, it is best to share authentic stories from your own life. Authentic stories help build connections. Make sure your stories are developmentally appropriate for your children. Avoid "make me" language like, "It makes me happy when my daughter..." Instead you might say, "I felt happy when my daughter..." Examples of happy stories to share include incidents from family vacations like when you all got wet on the log flume at the amusement park, reaching a goal like finishing a half-marathon, events like gathering with friends for a baby shower or an achievement like learning to make a fancy meal.

Adaptations for Younger Students: Remember it is important for young children to share their meaningful experiences with adults. If time is critical, review the suggestions in the "Getting Started" section on page viii.

Does anyone else want to share a story about a time they felt happy? Give Happy to the child who is sharing and use it as a talking indicator to show whose turn it is to speak. When finished speaking, this child gives Happy to the next speaker. If sharing the happy Feeling Buddy causes a commotion, use a talking stick to designate the speaker. If the child says, "It makes me happy when ___." Say, "You feel happy when ___" or "You felt happy when ___."

Look at Happy's eyebrows. They are going like this. Demonstrate.
Look at Happy's mouth. It is going like this. Demonstrate.
Now, make your face look like Happy's face. Notice children's expressions. (Read the Conscious Discipline tip below as you notice expressions.)
You did it! Your eyebrows are going like this. Demonstrate.
Your mouth is going like this. Demonstrate.
You seem happy, just like our new Feeling Buddy. Your faces look like this every day. It's exciting to see!

Conscious Discipline Tip: Noticing instead of judging is at the core of Conscious Discipline. Start your noticing sentences with the child's name, "you" or "your." Avoid saying "I noticed you ___." "I noticed" becomes about you and the child's relationship and leads to approval seeking. "Your face is going like this" is about the child and leads to conscious awareness.

Happy: Hi everyone! I'm so happy to meet you and be with you. We will have fun together! You know what I like to say a lot? Yahoo, look at you. Happy, happy, clap, one, two. Say it with me and clap your hands! Point to the words you wrote on sentence strips or chart paper as you all repeat Happy's chant. Place Happy in your lap.

I have another question for you. Have you ever felt sad? Bring out the sad Feeling Buddy and hold it up next to your face as you share a personal story. One time I felt sad when...

Does anyone want to share a story about a time you felt sad? Give Sad to the child who is sharing to use as a talking indicator like you did with Happy. Alternately, you may use a talking stick to designate the speaker instead of Sad, or pair off and use the Turn and Talk sticks.

Look at Sad's eyebrows. They are going like this. Demonstrate.
Look at Sad's mouth. It is going like this. Demonstrate.
Can you make your face look like Sad's face? Notice children's expressions.
You did it! Your eyebrows are going like this. Demonstrate.
Your mouth is going like this. Demonstrate.
You seem sad, just like our new Feeling Buddy. There are times I have seen this look on your faces, just like there are times I've seen your happy faces.

Sad: Hi, my name is Sad. I help people when they lose something they love. I will help you, too. I am going to say a chant. You are going to repeat it. Point to the words you wrote on sentence strips or chart paper as Sad chants:
Boo hoo, I see you.
When you feel sad, I will help you.
Hug Sad and tell children to hug themselves. Repeat the chant with the children. Put Sad in your lap.

I'm going to teach you a new song about feeling happy and feeling sad.

Sing: "Look at My Face Part 1" #19
Listen to the song and watch the instructional DVD. Sing *a cappella* using only Happy and Sad. After you introduce Angry and Scared play the CD.

Buddy Tip: It is helpful to begin by singing the two verses of the song that relate to happy and sad alone, and then add the music later.

Happy: Bye, everyone. Yahoo, look at you. Happy, happy, clap, one, two.

Sad: Bye bye! Boo hoo, I see you. When you feel sad, I will help you.

Happy and Sad live in these pockets. Show children the Feeling Buddies pockets. Put Happy and Sad in their places. **Look boys and girls, their names are on their pockets.** Point to the words and read the names with the children.

Hang the Feeling Buddy pocket chart in the circle area so you can refer to it. If a child is feeling happy or sad during the day say, "I noticed your eyebrows are like this (pull out Happy or Sad and point), your eyes are like this and your mouth is like this. Your face looks likes (Happy or Sad)." Do not put the Feeling Buddies in the Safe Place until after Lesson 2.4.

We have met two of our eight new friends. Once we meet all eight of them, they will help us be loving and kind to each other.

 Sing: "Bye, Bye Buddies" #4

 Adaptations for Younger Students: Unit 1 introduces all eight Buddies. For young children, you may choose to introduce and use only four of the Feeling Buddies. You can introduce the "cousins" later in the year.

Commitment:
In future units, you will make a verbal commitment with your students at the end of each lesson. During the first unit, however, the commitment is a written one for you to undertake on your own. Commitments create a mind-body biochemistry that helps us focus our attention and achieve our goals. Making a commitment verbally or on paper increases the likelihood of following through successfully. If you agree to each lesson's commitment in Unit 1, sign the space below it.

I commit to noticing at least three children per day when they are experiencing the feelings "happy" or "sad". I will notice and coach them using the DNA process taught on pages 79 and 82 in *Managing Emotional Mayhem*.

Signed: _____

Buddy Tip: You've already read about being a S.T.A.R. in *Managing Emotional Mayhem*, but here's a quick reminder: "S.T.A.R." is an acronym for **S**mile, **T**ake a deep breath **A**nd **R**elax. When you take three breaths using deep belly breathing, you help turn off the stress response in the body. We will go further in depth with this active calming skill later in the *Curriculum*, but you can begin using it today.

Extension Activities

Younger (Pre-K-Kindergarten)

How Do You Think You Would Feel? Prepare Happy/Sad sticks ahead of time by sticking happy and sad stickers back to back on the end of a popsicle stick. Give one Happy/Sad stick to each child. Share examples of situations that occur daily in your classroom. For example, "A friend takes your crayons. How do you think you would feel?" Coach students to use their Happy/Sad sticks to show the feeling. Make sure the examples relate specifically to happy and sad as best as possible. Repeat this activity with pairings of other feelings as you meet more Feeling Buddies.

 Conscious Discipline Tip: It is critical that you ask the question, "How do you think you would feel," instead of saying, "How do you think that would make you feel." Self-regulation requires children learn to own their feelings. Attributing the cause of their feelings to outside situations or people by using "make you" language yields blame and derails the process.

Play "What's Alike/What's Different": Hold up Happy and Sad together. Ask students, **What is alike? What is different? What do you notice?** Work with a partner, have students take turns making either a happy or sad face. What is the difference?

Arts and Crafts: Print reproducibles 1.1 A "Happy Face" and 1.1 B "Sad Face." Glue colored yarn in place for mouths and eyebrows. Glue googly eyes in place for the eyes. When the glue dries, children can run their hands over the faces in a kinesthetic activity.

Older (First and Second Grades)

Writing Prompts: Create writing prompts for students. "We've all had times when we've felt _____. Think about a time when you felt _____. Now, write and illustrate about one time when you felt _____." This is a great opportunity to offer a choice: **You have a choice! You may write about feeling happy or you may write about feeling sad. Which is best for you?**

Older (Third to Fifth Grades)

Writing Prompts: Create writing prompts for students. "We've all had times when we've felt _____. Think about a time when you felt _____. Now, write about one time when you felt _____." This is a great opportunity to offer a choice: **You have a choice! You may write about feeling happy or you may write about feeling sad. Which is best for you?**

Hello, Angry and Scared

Goal: To identify and name facial cues for the emotional states of angry and scared

Materials

- ☐ *Listen to Your Feelings* CD Songs:
  - "It's Buddy Time" #16
  - "Look at My Face Part 1" #19
  - "Bye, Bye Buddies" #4
- ☐ Happy and Sad Feeling Buddies in their pockets
- ☐ Angry and Scared Feeling Buddies
- ☐ Reproducibles
  - 1.2 A (optional, all ages)
  - 1.2 B, 1.2 C, 1.2 D (optional, younger)
  - 1.2 E (optional, older)
- ☐ S.T.A.R. icon
- ☐ Chart paper or sentence strips
- ☐ Markers or crayons (optional, younger)
- ☐ Turn and Talk sticks (optional)
- ☐ Talking stick (optional)
- ☐ Happy/Sad sticks (optional, younger)
- ☐ Yarn, googly eyes, crayons (optional, younger)
- ☐ Happy and Sad chants on sentence strips from Lesson 1.1
- ☐ Instructional DVD

Word Wall

Angry, Scared

Before You Begin

- Gather materials
- Write Angry and Scared's chants on sentence strips or chart paper
- Watch the songs for Lesson 1.2 by selecting "Circle Time" then "Songs By Lesson" on your instructional DVD
- Print your reproducibles
- Prepare a Feelings Language Chart (optional)
- **Word Wall:** Angry, Scared

Let's Get Started

 Sing: "It's Buddy Time" #16

Continue to keep the new Feeling Buddies hidden behind your back, under a blanket or in a basket until you introduce them at the beginning of each lesson. This will create a predictable and exciting routine for the children in which they can anticipate meeting more new Feeling Buddy friends.

Do you remember which Buddies we have already met?
We met Happy. Take Happy out of the pocket.

Happy: Yahoo, look at you. Happy, happy, clap, one, two.
Point to the chant you wrote on sentence strips or chart paper.

We met Sad. Take Sad out of the pocket.

Sad: Boo hoo, I see you. When you feel sad, I will help you.
Point to the chant you wrote on sentence strips or chart paper.

Today we are going to meet two more Buddies. Hold up the Feeling Buddy named Scared. What do you think this Feeling Buddy's name could be?

 Buddy Tip: Be certain to use the gender-neutral term "it" when talking about the Buddies. Assigning a gender labels the feelings as a "boy" or "girl" issue and may impede children's ability to relate.

Look at Scared's eyebrows. They are going like this. Demonstrate.
Look at Scared's mouth. It is going like this. Demonstrate.
Make your face look like Scared's face.
You did it! Your eyebrows are going like this. Demonstrate.
Your mouth is going like this. Demonstrate.
You seem scared, and this Feeling Buddy's name is Scared. There are times I have seen this look on your faces, just like there are times I've seen your happy and sad faces!

One time I felt scared when… Share a personal story. Hold Scared next to your face as you share your story.

 **Buddy Tip:** Examples of scary stories include the time when you had to stop the car suddenly and were afraid you were going to hit the car in front of you, the time your young son wandered off at the mall and you were afraid you'd lost him or the time you went to the top of the Empire State Building and were afraid because you were very high up.

Does anyone want to share a story about a time you felt scared? Give Scared to the child who is sharing, use a talking stick to designate the speaker or use the Turn and Talk sticks as described in "Getting Started."

Scared: Hi, my name is Scared. You know what I like to say a lot?
Oh my, fear, fear, fear.
Seek safety, there's a Safekeeper near!

Point to the chant you wrote on sentence strips or chart paper. Lead children in repeating the chant. Place Scared in your lap.

Hold up the Feeling Buddy named Angry. **What do you think this Feeling Buddy's name could be?**

Look at Angry's eyebrows. **They are going like this.** Demonstrate while holding Angry by your face.

Look at Angry's mouth. It is going like this. Demonstrate.

Can you make your face look like Angry's face?

You did it! Your eyebrows are going like this. Demonstrate.

Your mouth is going like this. Demonstrate.

You seem angry and this Feeling Buddy's name is Angry.

Does anyone want to share a story about a time you felt angry? Listen to one or two stories.

Angry: Hey, hey my name is Angry. You know what I like to say a lot?
I'll rant and I'll rave.
Something's bugging me!
Nothing will change until I breathe.

Point to the chant you wrote on sentence strips or chart paper. Lead children in repeating the chant.

Boys and girls, let's <u>S</u>top, <u>T</u>ake a deep breath <u>A</u>nd <u>R</u>elax to see if we can help calm Angry now.

Angry: Whew, that helps. May I go back into my pocket home?

Yes, you may. Place Angry in its pocket home.

Scared: What about me? What about me? I want my pocket home, too!

Here you go, Scared. Cuddle up safely in your pocket. Place Scared in its pocket home. **You're safe. We will keep you safe.**

We are going to sing the song we learned yesterday, but we are going to add verses about Scared and Angry.

 Sing: "Look at My Face Part 1" #19

Sing along to all four verses for happy, sad, angry and scared. Point to each Buddy or hold it up as you sing about it and then put it back into its pocket home.

Now we have met four Feeling Buddies: Happy, Sad, Angry and Scared. Do you think there are any more Feeling Buddies to meet? Point to the empty pockets. **We'll have to wait and see.**

 Sing: "Bye, Bye Buddies" #4

Commitment: I commit to noticing at least three children per day when they are experiencing the feelings of anger or fear. I will notice and coach them using the DNA process taught on pages 71 and 75 in *Managing Emotional Mayhem*.

Signed: _____

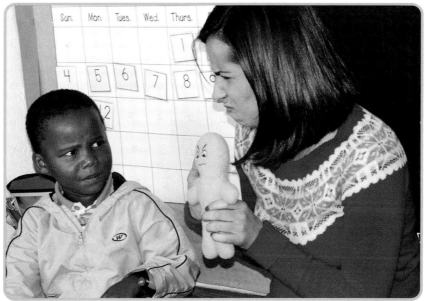

Extension Activities

All Ages

Feelings Language Chart
Prepare a Feelings Language Chart using the writing frame: (Student's name) felt angry (or scared) when (describe the event).

Coach each student to write or dictate an ending to the sentence. Read through the chart as a group once you have completed it. For younger children, it is helpful to conduct this activity in small groups.

Look at My Face #1 Book
Take photos or have older students take photos of each other with happy, sad, angry and scared expressions on their faces. Bind the photos together in a "Look at My Face #1" class book using reproducible 1.2 A "Look at My Face." Help younger students fill in the blanks.

Younger

Arts and Crafts
Print reproducibles 1.2 B "Angry Face" and 1.2 C "Scared Face." Glue colored yarn in place for mouths and eyebrows. Glue googly eyes in place for the eyes. When the glue dries, children can run their hands over the faces in a kinesthetic activity.

My New Friends
Print reproducible 1.2 D "My New Friends" and have children draw the faces.

Older

Writing Prompts
Create writing prompts for students. "We've all had times when we've felt _____. Think about a time when you felt _____. Now, write about one time when you felt _____."

My New Friends
Print reproducible 1.2 E "My New Friends." Children will illustrate the faces and write the names of the four Feeling Buddies.

If you are teaching Pre-K or younger wait until later in the year to introduce the other Feeling Buddies (Frustrated, Disappointed, Anxious and Calm). You can use binding clips to fold the Feeling Buddy pockets up to hide Calm, Disappointed, Anxious and Frustrated. Take time to play guessing games with the Buddies to help students practice identifying them by their faces. For example, hide one of the four Buddies behind your back and sing, "Who is missing? Let me see. Can it be?" (Sing to the tune of *Frère Jacques*). When children guess, place them in the correct pocket.

Hello, Calm and Disappointed

Goal: To identify and name facial cues for the emotional states of calm and disappointed

Materials

- ❏ *Listen to Your Feelings* CD
  Songs:
  - "It's Buddy Time" #16
  - "Look at My Face
    Part 1" #19
  - "Look at My Face
    Part 2" #20
  - "Bye, Bye Buddies" #4
- ❏ Feeling Buddy pockets containing Happy, Sad, Angry and Scared
- ❏ Calm and Disappointed Feeling Buddies
- ❏ Clear plastic bottle, water, food coloring
- ❏ All previous chants or sentence strips
- ❏ Instructional DVD

Word Wall

Calm, Disappointed, Cousin

Before You Begin

- Gather materials
- Write Calm and Disappointed's chants on sentence strips or chart paper
- Make a Feelings Bottle: Partially fill a clear plastic bottle with water. Use a few drops of food coloring to dye the water for better visibility. You will use the Feelings Bottle to represent the physiological aspects of emotional upset in a form children can understand.
- Watch the songs for Lesson 1.3 by selecting "Circle Time" then "Songs By Lesson" on your instructional DVD
- **Word Wall:** Calm, Disappointed, Cousin

Let's Get Started

 Sing: "It's Buddy Time" #16

Continue to hide the new Feeling Buddies until you introduce them in the lesson. This creates a predictable and exciting routine for the children.

Do you remember when we first met Happy and Sad? Hold up Happy and Sad and place them back into their pocket homes.

Happy: Yahoo, look at you. Happy, happy, clap, one, two.
Say it with me and clap your hands. Watch me. I'll show you:
Yahoo, look at you. Happy, happy, clap, one, two.

Sad: Boo hoo, I see you. When you feel sad, I'm here to help you.

Today we are going to meet their cousins. Do you have a cousin?

I have a cousin named Cindy. In some ways we are very much alike and in some ways we are a little bit different. When Cindy is happy, she is really, really happy. She jumps around, laughing and giggling. Sometimes it is hard for her to sit still. Demonstrate by jumping around happily. Move Happy so it is jumping up and down also. Have you ever been happy like that?

I also feel happy, but my happy looks different. I look like this. Demonstrate a calm face. I have a Feeling Buddy just like me. Show the calm Feeling Buddy. This is Happy's cousin, Calm.

Sometimes my face looks like Calm's when I look up at the clouds or watch my children sleep. Have you ever felt peaceful and quietly happy like Calm?

Show the children the Feelings Bottle. Hold it still and horizontal to the ground. When we feel calm our insides feel just like this. We feel peaceful and all is well.

Look at Calm's eyebrows. They are going like this. Demonstrate while holding Calm next to your face. Look at Calm's mouth. It is going like this. Demonstrate.
Can you make your face look like Calm's face? Notice children's responses.
You did it! Your eyebrows are going like this. Demonstrate.
Your mouth is going like this. Demonstrate.
You seem calm and this Feeling Buddy's name is Calm.

Calm: Hello everybody. My name is Calm. Do you know what I like to say a lot? Wait! First I'm going to take a deep breath, and then I can say it. Here it goes: Ahhhhh. All is well.

Lead children in taking a deep belly breath and repeating the chant.

Do you remember when we met Sad? Well, Disappointed is Sad's cousin. Sometimes when it was time for Cindy to go home, I would feel sad. When I felt sad, I got kind of quiet and I looked like this. Tears ran down my cheeks. Demonstrate sad.

But when it was time to leave, Cindy's shoulders slumped like this and her face looked like this. Demonstrate disappointment. Cindy felt disappointed we had to stop playing. She was hoping we could play longer. I felt sad because playtime was over, and Cindy felt disappointed.

This is Disappointed. Hold up the disappointed Feeling Buddy next to your face.
Look at Disappointed's eyebrows. They are going like this. Demonstrate.
Look at Disappointed's mouth. It is going like this. Demonstrate.
Can you make your face look like Disappointed's face? Notice children's responses.
You did it! Your eyebrows are going like this. Demonstrate.

Your mouth is going like this. Demonstrate.
You seem disappointed and this Feeling Buddy's name is Disappointed.

Have you ever felt disappointed? Maybe you thought something was going to happen and it didn't?
Maybe you were hoping you would get a toy at the store but your mom said, "No."
Maybe you wanted to watch a television show but it was time to go to bed.
Maybe you wanted to get picked first for the team but they picked someone else.
Use speaking props and strategies as needed for sharing.

Disappointed: Hi, my name is Disappointed. I was hoping you would meet me before my cousin, Sad, but I can handle it. You know what I like to say? I was hoping to get my way, But I can handle it.

Lead the class in repeating Disappointed's chant. Place Disappointed back in its pocket home.

Disappointed helps us learn how to handle times when things just don't go as we were hoping.

Conscious Discipline Tip: Instead of focusing on good and bad, shift your focus to behaviors that are helpful or hurtful. Notice children doing helpful acts in the classroom by saying, "You pushed your chair in so no one would trip over it. That was helpful." Or you might say, "Pushing in line is hurtful. What could you do that is helpful?"

Now we are going to sing our song, "Look at My Face," and add our new friends to the song. Pull each Feeling Buddy out of its pocket to display as you sing about that particular Buddy. It is best to begin by singing the verses without the music and to sing only about the Feeling Buddies you have met so far.

 Sing: "Look at My Face Part 1" #19 (optional) and "Look at My Face Part 2" #20

There are some empty pockets. Do you think we will meet more new friends?
We'll wait and see. Sometimes it's hard to wait!

Disappointed: Yeah, waiting can be a bummer. You can help me by saying, "You can handle it." Coach children to chant, **You can handle it.**

Thanks, that's really helpful!

 Sing: "Bye, Bye Buddies" #4

Commitment: I commit to noticing at least three children per day when they are experiencing the feelings "calm" or "disappointed." I will notice and coach them using the DNA process on pages 79 and 82 in *Managing Emotional Mayhem*.

Signed: _____

Extension Activities

Older

Writing Prompts

Create writing prompts for students. "We've all had times when we've felt _____. Think about a time when you felt _____. Now, write about one time when you felt _____."

Hello, Anxious and Frustrated

Goal: To identify and name facial cues for the emotional states of anxious and frustrated

Materials

- ❏ *Listen to Your Feelings* CD Songs:
  - "Buddy Helper" #3
  - "Look at My Face Part 2" #20
  - "Bye, Bye Buddies" #4
- ❏ Happy, Sad, Angry, Calm, Scared and Disappointed Feeling Buddies in their pockets
- ❏ Anxious and Frustrated Feeling Buddies
- ❏ Template
  - T.1 "Buddy Helper"
- ❏ Scissors (optional, younger)
- ❏ Reproducibles
  - 1.4 A (optional, younger)
  - 1.4 B, 1.4 C (optional, older)
- ❏ Instructional DVD

Word Wall

Anxious, Frustrated

Before You Begin

- Gather materials
- Print reproducibles
- Write Anxious and Frustrated's chants on sentence strips or chart paper
- Watch the songs for Lesson 1.4 by selecting "Circle Time" then "Songs By Lesson" on your instructional DVD
- Print and cut out your Buddy Helper job card using Template T.1
- Add the Buddy Helper to your class job list. If you add the Buddy Helper job now the job is to get the Buddies for teaching time. If you are in a classroom without a full-time assistant, you may want to wait and use this job for a child to help coach wtih the Buddies in the Safe Place. This will come after Lesson 4.4.
- **Word Wall:** Anxious, Frustrated

Let's Get Started

Continue to hide the new Feeling Buddies until you introduce them in the lesson. This creates a predictable and exciting routine for the children.

(Only do this if you are going to use the Buddy Helper job now. If not you can select a volunteer.)

Today we are going to learn a new song. As we sing the name of each Feeling Buddy, our Buddy Helper will point to the Buddy. The Buddy Helper is a new class job that will help us with our Buddies. Hold up the Buddy Helper job card.

Conscious Discipline Tip: In Conscious Discipline, everyone in the class has a job. If you are not familiar with Conscious Discipline and School Family™ Jobs, please refer to the book *Creating the School Family: Bully-Proofing Classrooms Through Emotional Intelligence* for assistance. If you have purchased a *School Family Job Set* from Conscious Discipline, print Template T.1, laminate it and add it to your job board.

Everyone will have a chance to be the Buddy Helper, just like everyone has a chance to do each of our other class jobs. You will know when it is your turn by looking at the School Family Job Board. I will tell you more about the Buddy Helper's duties as we need them.

 Sing: "Buddy Helper" #3

Do you remember when we met Happy and Sad? Point to the Buddies.
How about Scared and Angry? Point to the Buddies.
Do you remember Calm and Disappointed? Point to the Buddies.
Do you remember Happy and Sad's cousins? Ask a child to come up and find Happy's cousin.
Ask another child to find Sad's cousin.

Today we are going to meet two more cousins. I am going to tell two stories to introduce them. The first story is about a time I felt anxious. Anxious is Scared's cousin.

Hold up Anxious, share a personal example and contrast it with scared. Scared is about a real fear and anxious is about a made up fear. For example, you were afraid last summer when a dog chased you down the street. You are anxious about going to the dentist next week because you might have a cavity.

Do you have a story about a time you felt anxious?

Look at Anxious' eyebrows. They are going like this. Demonstrate while holding Anxious next to your face.
Look at Anxious' mouth. It is going like this. Demonstrate.
Can you make your face look like Anxious' face?
You did it! Your eyebrows are going like this. Demonstrate.
Your mouth is going like this. Demonstrate.
You seem anxious and this Feeling Buddy's name is Anxious.

Anxious: Hi, my name is Anxious. I was feeling anxious because I thought maybe you would not like me. My job is to help you get more information. I feel better just seeing your kind and smiling faces. You know what I like to say a lot? What, what will happen? I need to know!

Coach children to repeat the chant, then place Anxious in your lap.

Now, I will introduce you to the last Feeling Buddy named Frustrated. Frustrated is Angry's cousin. Hold up Frustrated. **Anger is usually directed at someone else. Frustration is usually directed at ourselves or at the circumstances of the situation.**

 Adaptations for Younger Students: If you choose to introduce the cousins, simplify the wording. Saying, "Anger points to someone else. Frustration points to me or what is happening to me," will make the concept easier for young children to understand.

Contrast Angry and Frustrated like we have done in the other "cousin" lessons. Share a personal example of a time you felt frustrated. You might share a story about a time you felt frustrated at school. For example, "Remember when the puzzles were all dumped out and how difficult it was to figure out which pieces went with what puzzle? I felt frustrated. Now I have labeled the back of each piece so next time it will be easier to figure out."

Do you have a story about a time when you felt frustrated? You were trying to do something and it was really hard and nothing you did seemed to work? Use speaking props and strategies for sharing.

Look at Frustrated's eyebrows. They are going like this. Demonstrate while holding Frustrated next to your face.
Look at Frustrated's mouth. It is going like this. Demonstrate.
Can you make your face look like Frustrated's face?
You did it! Your eyebrows are going like this. Demonstrate.
Your mouth is going like this. Demonstrate.
You seem frustrated and this Feeling Buddy's name is Frustrated.

Frustrated: Hi, my name is Frustrated. You know what I like to say a lot? I'll huff and puff because I've had enough.

Coach children to repeat the chant and point to where you wrote it on sentence strips or chart paper.

You can help me by saying, "Breathe with me, would you like some help?" Lead the class in being a S.T.A.R. and saying, "Breathe with me, would you like some help?"

Frustrated: Whew, I feel better now. No thanks on the help, just put me back in my pocket please.

Distribute the Buddies to eight different children. Instruct children to listen to the song and place each Buddy in its corresponding pocket when the song sings its name. Instruct the remaining children to make the facial expression that corresponds with the Buddy.

If you don't have a Buddy, you still have a job. Your job is to make the face of the feeling as each Buddy goes back into its pocket home.

 Sing: "Look at My Face Part 1" #19 (optional) and "Look at My Face Part 2" #20

We're going to use these Feeling Buddies every day. Sometimes it will be hard to put them away. It will be the Buddy Helper's job to help us put our Buddies away by giving a thumbs up each time someone puts a Buddy in the correct home. If someone chooses the wrong pocket, the Buddy Helper can say, "Oops, try again" or "Let me help you," and point to the correct pocket. (Student name) is our Buddy Helper today.

 Buddy Tip: Role-play putting a Buddy in the wrong pocket and coach the Buddy Helper in saying both, "Oops, try again" and "Let me help you," while pointing to the correct pocket.

Put the Buddy Helper job card in your job board with the student's name. If necessary, explain which jobs you combined to make room for the new Buddy Helper job.

Let's sing the "Bye, Bye Buddies" song. Remove the Buddies and hand them to eight children to put away. Have the Buddy Helper stand by the pocket board and check the placement of each Buddy.

 Sing: "Bye, Bye Buddies" #4

Commitment: I commit to noticing at least three children per day when they are experiencing the feelings "frustrated" or "anxious." I will notice and coach them using the DNA process on pages 72 and 76 in *Managing Emotional Mayhem*.

Signed: _____

Extension Activities

Younger (Pre-K–Kindergarten)

Who is Missing? Print reproducible 1.4 A "Who is Missing?" Children can cut out the Buddies at the bottom of the page or you can precut the Buddies for them. For the activity, children decide who is missing and glue the missing Buddy in place. Encourage children to take the reproducible home to share what they have learned about their Feeling Buddies with their families.

Older

Who is Missing? Hand out reproducible 1.4 B "Who is Missing?" Students will decide who is missing, and then draw the missing Buddy and write its name in the appropriate space. Encourage children to take the reproducible home to share what they have learned about their Feeling Buddies with their families.

My Friends and Cousins: Print reproducible 1.4 C "Cousins," and have children draw the faces and write the names.

Comparing Cousins (K-2): Print large feeling faces for two cousins (Scared and Anxious). Tape them to the top of chart paper and draw a line down the middle. Have students compare and contrast the two feelings. Scared and anxious are similiar feelings, yet they are different. When you feel scared, you have a real fear. When you feel anxious, you have a made up fear. Think about a time you felt scared. Now, think about a time you felt anxious. How were your feelings the same? How were they different? Chart student responses.

Comparative Writing (3-5): Create a comparative writing prompt for older students. "Scared and anxious are similar feelings, yet they are different. When you feel scared, you have a real fear. When you feel anxious, you have a made up fear. Think about a time you felt scared. Now, think about a time you felt anxious. Write about those times, describing what happened and how you felt. How were your feelings the same? How were your feelings different?" You can make similar prompts for all the primary feelings and cousins.

When I Feel ___, My Face Looks Like This

Goal: Recognizing and naming feeling faces

Materials

- *Listen to Your Feelings* CD Songs:
  - "Hello Buddies" #9
  - "Bye, Bye Buddies" #4
- Feeling Buddies in their buddy pockets
- Basket of Buddies
- Reproducibles
  - 1.5 A (all ages)
  - 1.5 B, 1.5 C, 1.5 D, 1.5 E (younger)
- Markers or crayons
- Hand-held mirrors (optional)
- Soft music to work to (optional)
- Instructional DVD

Before You Begin

- Gather materials
- Select a container for the Buddies who don't live in the pocket board
- Watch the songs for Lesson 1.5 by selecting "Circle Time" then "Songs By Lesson" on your instructional DVD
- Print reproducibles

Let's Get Started

 Sing: "Hello Buddies" #9

We have met eight new friends lately; they are our Feeling Buddies and they live in their pocket homes. The Buddies in their pocket homes will soon live in a very important place in our classroom. We will learn about that important place next week. (You may say in a few days depending on how quickly you plan to move through the *Curriculum*.)

We also have another set of Feeling Buddies. This is their home. Hold up the extra set of Buddies in the storage container you have chosen to use for them.

This is our basket of Buddies. We have a total of two of each of our Buddies. Let's look at them all. Instruct the Buddy Helper to pull the Buddies out of the basket one at a time. Instruct the children to name the Buddy as the helper pulls each one out.

Buddy Tip: Store the set of Buddies who don't live in the pocket board in a container they can stay in all year long. A basket makes an ideal Buddy holder because you can see all their expressions for easy access. For this reason, we will use the term "basket of Buddies" to refer to these Buddies in the remaining lessons.

Now let's look at our cousins. Hold up Angry and Frustrated. **Can you see the difference between Angry and Frustrated? How can we tell one from the other?** Repeat with all the cousins.

You looked carefully and noticed that the Buddies' faces are different. Today, we are going to start making a class book called "Our Feeling Faces." It will take three steps.

Conscious Discipline Tip: We often say, "Good job!" or "Thank you!" when children comply with our commands. These types of statements teach children to follow rules in order to please the adult. In Conscious Discipline the goal is not to please others, but to foster safety and build intrinsic motivation. Acknowledge children's efforts and compliance by saying, "You did it!" or "Good for you!"

First, you are going to think about a time you had a strong feeling. You could have felt really happy, really scared, really angry or really sad. Or maybe you felt like one of the feeling cousins. Second, you are going to give your feeling a name and write it on your book page. Third, you are going to draw a picture of what you think your face might have looked like.

Hold up reproducible 1.5 A "When I Feel" so the students can see where to write the feeling name and where to draw the feeling face. (This activity is for Kindergarten and older. You may need to write the feeling name on your student's book page. If you teach Pre-K please see the adaptation for younger students below.)

First, you are going to choose a feeling.

Then you are going to write the name of your feeling in this blank: When I feel _____ my face looks like this. Point to the blank.

Last, you are going to draw your face in the big empty circle. Point to the circle. You can use the Buddies to help you draw.

Buddy Tip: You may want to provide hand-held mirrors so children can see their own faces and expressions to help them draw.

See if you can remember the three steps: Write the steps on the board or draw pictures for younger children.

1. Think of a time you felt a really, really strong feeling.
2. Give the feeling a name and write it on the paper. Point to the blank.
3. Draw what your face looked like. Point to the circle.

Do you have any questions?

Play soft music as children work (optional). Bind the book together when the children are finished. Place the book in the class library for children to read over and over again.

Adaptations for Younger Students: You will distribute reproducible 1.5 B, 1.5 C, 1.5 D or 1.5 E to each child to match the feeling he or she chooses. Change the instructions from "give the feeling a name and write it on the paper" to "give the feeling a name and tell it to me" so you can give each child the corresponding reproducible.

 Sing: "Bye, Bye Buddies" #4

Buddy Tip: Periodically use the following songs with the Buddies to reinforce facial recognition of the feelings and practice naming them. Watch your instructional DVD to see how to sing the songs and for examples of the wonderful interactions the Buddies provide: "Hello Buddies," "We All Feel" circle chant, "Move to the Feelings," "Do You Know," and the "Clap and Feel" partner game.

Commitment: I commit to noticing at least three children per day when they are experiencing any of the feelings we have discussed in Unit 1. I will notice them with a description of their facial expression, not a judgment of their feeling state or actions, by using these words: "Your face is going like this (demonstrate). You seem _____, like our _____ Feeling Buddy (point to the Buddy)."

Signed: _____

Resources

Managing Emotional Mayhem
- Chapter 3: Feeling Messages: Following Our Emotional Guidance System

Creating the School Family
- Chapter 5: The Safekeeper
- Chapter 11: Classroom Jobs

Shubert's School on ConsciousDiscipline.com/Shubert
- Click the Job Chart to see how teachers are implementing jobs in their classrooms.
- Click the S.T.A.R. wand to view videos of children being a S.T.A.R.

School Family Job Set
- Provide you the structure and information to give a job for every class member.

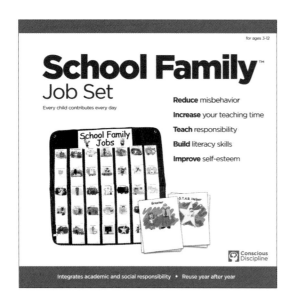

School Family Job Set

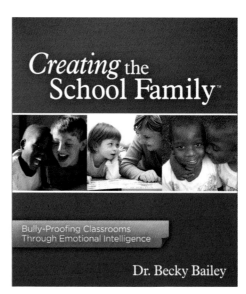

Creating the School Family

I Am: Acting Out My Emotions

Anger Gets Ahold of Me

Goal: To understand that when we first feel an emotion such as anger, it takes over our thoughts, feelings and actions, and hijacks our ability to problem-solve

Materials

- *Listen to Your Feelings* CD Songs:
  - "Buddy Helper" #3
  - "Anger Got Ahold of Me" #1
- Angry Feeling Buddy
- Reproducibles
  - 2.1 A (optional, younger)
  - 2.1 B, 2.1 C (optional, older)
  - 2.1 D
- *I Am Upset Smock*
- Shubert Bug Crazy Mad picture
- S.T.A.R. icon
- Feelings Bottle
- *Managing Emotional Mayhem*
- Instructional DVD

Word Wall

Commitment

Before You Begin

- Watch the "Step 1: I Am" video in the "Five Steps to Self-Regulation" section on your instructional DVD
- Watch the songs for Lesson 2.1 by selecting "Circle Time" then "Songs By Lesson" on your instructional DVD
- Gather materials
- Review *Managing Emotional Mayhem*, Chapter 5
- **Word Wall:** Commitment

Let's Get Started

 Sing: "Buddy Helper" #3

Use this story or an anger story that feels real to you:

The other day I wanted to go see a special movie with a friend. I felt so excited about the movie! I wanted to see the whole movie from the beginning to the end. As we were leaving her house, my friend kept forgetting things and running back in to get her purse, her sweater and the car keys.

I felt my insides getting angry like a volcano that was going to erupt. I yelled, "Hurry up! Hurry up! We are going to the miss the movie!" I felt my face getting hot. We arrived to the theater late. The movie had already started. I was angry, really really angry.

My face looked like this. Purse your lips, furrow your brow. My body looked like this. Ball up your fists, cross your arms.

My voice sounded like this, "I told you we would be late! I hate being late!"
My whole body was tight and it looked like this. Demonstrate.
I was angry. Anger got ahold of me. Put on the angry *I Am Upset Smock*.

What I wanted even changed. Instead of wanting to see the movie, I wanted to be mean and hurtful to my friend. Can you think of a time when anger got ahold of you?

Buddy Tip: Authentic stories convey the most powerful messages. For best results, choose a story from your life that mimics this "movie" story. What happened the last time you felt angry? Avoid "make me" language by saying, "I felt angry when _____," and be certain children can relate to the story you choose. Possible examples might include a time when a friend borrowed a special outfit and got a stain on it, when you planned to go on vacation but your flight was cancelled, or the time your dog peed on your new carpet.

Put the angry *I Am Upset Smock* on children as they share. Coach them to show how their faces looked, how their hands looked, how their voices changed and whether they changed their goals from getting something they wanted to hurting someone. Follow up with a summary statement using variations of the sentence, "So when your brother pushed you down the stairs, anger got ahold of you!" If possible, divide your class into subgroups with an aid or assistant so everyone can share. If you don't have time for everyone to share, revisit this lesson later to give everyone an opportunity.

Anger gets ahold of us all. When it does, it takes over our whole body. Our insides feel like this. Hold up and shake the Feelings Bottle.

Anger takes over your whole body. Your face will look like this. Coach children to make angry faces.
Your hands may look like this. Coach the whole class to make their hands into angry fists.
Your arms may look like this. Coach the whole class in crossing their arms in front of their bodies.
Your voice might sound like this. Coach the whole class in angrily screaming, "You're mean, I don't like you anymore."
Your body may look like this. Coach the whole class to stand strong and stomp their feet or make a fist.
You might want to hit, push or grab. Act out the motions for each of the words.

Adaptations for Younger Students: Change the angry statement to, "Stop it, you are not my friend," instead of, "Shut up..." or choose another phrase you commonly hear in the classroom.

When anger gets ahold of us, we cannot think. We cannot remember how to solve problems. We feel out of control on the inside. Shake the feelings bottle again. I was so angry with my friend for being late that I didn't pay attention to the movie at all!

I was bug crazy mad and I could be hurtful! Hold up the Shubert Bug Crazy Mad picture provided in your *Toolkit*. Explain to children angry and mad are two words that mean the same thing. When I get really angry, it's like I am lost in anger. Angry takes over and Ms. Becky (insert your own name) disappears. Put on the angry *I Am Upset Smock*. Shake a couple of children's hands and introduce yourself. Hi, my new name is Anger. Hello, I am Angry. Nice to meet you. Anger got ahold of me. I am not Ms. Becky anymore, I am Angry!

 Conscious Discipline Tip: "Bug crazy mad" is a phrase from *Shubert is a S.T.A.R.*, one of seven children's literature titles by Dr. Becky Bailey. In *Shubert is a S.T.A.R.*, an upset in class triggers bug crazy anger! Mrs. Bookbinder uses the opportunity to teach active calming strategies and introduce the Safe Place. If you are new to Conscious Discipline, purchasing and reading the Shubert books will introduce you and the children to the Seven Basic Skills that are needed to handle all discipline situations.

Angry: Hey, you can't be Angry. That is my name. You can't be me! Are you lost? Where is Ms. Becky? Where did she go? You better get her back real soon. I can be hurtful if you let me take over!

Someone bugged me and I was late to see my movie.

Angry: Well you still can't be me. You better find yourself before you let me hurt someone. Learn to be a S.T.A.R. Do it now with me. Smile, Take a deep breath And Relax. Then you can help me. I don't like hurting people. I need your help. So, breathe and help me. Breathing is like hitting the pause button so you can take off the smock, calm down and be yourself again. (If you have taught Stop, Take a deep breath And Relax, explain that when you smile it will help relax and change your inner state.)

 **Buddy Tip:** S.T.A.R. is an acronym commonly mentioned in Conscious Discipline. Sometimes it is used for "Stop, Take a deep breath And Relax," and sometimes it's used for "Smile, Take a deep breath And Relax." Each use has benefits. Say, "Stop," when you want to cease an impulse. Say, "Smile," when you want to encourage a relaxed inner state. It is important to encourage children to take three deep breaths to calm down their nervous system.

Class, let's try this together. Let's all <u>S</u>mile, <u>T</u>ake a deep breath <u>A</u>nd <u>R</u>elax and see what happens. Put down the picture.

Wow, it is working! Let's do it again. Shake the Feelings Bottle and then let it settle into a calm state. **Much much better. One more time.** Take off the angry *I Am Upset Smock* and continue in an excited tone.

It worked! It worked! I'm back and now I can think of helpful ways to solve my problems. Hello children, my name is Ms. Becky. Glad to be back with you.

Whew! Now I can think about how to solve my problems in a helpful way. I have an idea. I could have helped my friend get ready faster before the movie instead of just yelling, "Hurry up, hurry up." I could have said, "How can I help you so we can be on time to the movie?"
Let's practice having anger get ahold of us and then helping each other calm down by being a S.T.A.R.

 Adaptations for Younger Students: You may want to take more than one day to teach this lesson and teach only one verse of "Anger Got Ahold of Me" per day. You may also wish to break into small groups when you are ready for them to put on the *I Am Upset Smock*.

Select a child to act out the song using the smock and other props. Encourage the rest of the class to act out "Anger Got Ahold of Me" without props. Model this first with a student before playing the song and having children do it with a partner. It's important to model this so children know how to play and keep it safe. Have children get with a partner. Have the child with the longest hair be Angry. They will "Get ahold of their partner." The first verse they pull away and struggle with Angry. The second and third verse they look at Angry, hold their hands and breathe.

Verse 1: (Before playing the song demonstrate using the props below, then have children partner up.)
I'm coloring with my marker.
Someone grabs it away from me. Put the angry *I Am Upset Smock* on the child.
My eyes look mean. My hands make a fist. Shake the Feelings Bottle.
Anger got ahold of me. Show the Bug Crazy Mad picture.
Class chants twice: **Anger got ahold of you. Anger got ahold of you.** Have a child hold up a large pause button (2.1 D).

Angry: Hey you can't be me. Better be a S.T.A.R.
Hold up the icon for S.T.A.R. breathing and have the children breathe deeply and slowly three times. As this happens, have the child remove the angry smock, show the water in the bottle settling from agitated to flat, put aside the Shubert Bug Crazy Mad picture and have the child shout, "I'm back!"

Buddy Tip: To designate it's time for S.T.A.R. breathing, you can use the S.T.A.R. icon or the *Safe Place Mat*, or purchase a star wand from a discount store.

Verse 2:

I'm walking down the hall.

Someone pushed me out of the way. Put the angry *I Am Upset Smock* on another child.

My heart beats fast. I clenched my teeth. Shake the Feelings Bottle.

Anger got ahold of me. Show the Bug Crazy Mad picture.

Class chants twice: Anger got ahold of you. Anger got ahold of you.

Angry: Hey you can't be me. I am me and you are you. Better be a S.T.A.R.

Hold up pause button. Hold up an icon for S.T.A.R. breathing and have the children breathe with and for the angry child three times. As this happens, have the child remove the angry smock, set aside the Bug Crazy Mad picture, let the Feelings Bottle settle and shout, "I'm back!"

Verse 3:

I was watching my favorite show.

My sister changed the channel. Put the angry *I Am Upset Smock* on the child.

I wanted to push. I wanted to hit. Shake the Feelings Bottle.

Anger got ahold of me. Show the Bug Crazy Mad picture.

Class chants twice: Anger got ahold of you. Anger got ahold of you.

Angry: Hey you can't be me. I am me, and you are you. Better be a S.T.A.R.

Hold up pause button. Hold up an icon for S.T.A.R. breathing and have the children breathe with and for the angry child three times. As this happens, have the child remove the angry smock, set aside the Bug Crazy Mad picture, calm the Feelings Bottle and have the child shout, "I'm back!"

Lead the children in acting out the verses in the song as they sing.

 Sing: "Anger Got Ahold of Me" #1

Commitment: This week we are going to practice two things. First, we are going to notice when anger gets ahold of us. Second, we are going to practice being a S.T.A.R. Make this commitment with me by taking three deep breaths. 1-2-3.

Extension Activities

Younger (Pre-K - First Grade)

Taking the Smock Off

(This reproducible is helpful to have children keep and review to help them remember how to take off the smock.) Have each child complete reproducible 2.1 A "Taking the Smock Off" by filling in their names in the "Hello, my name is _____," space and drawing a picture of themselves above their names.

Older

What Helps You Get Back to Calm

Use reproducible 2.1 B "What Helps to Calm" to reaffirm the ways children can calm down when anger gets a hold of them. Children will write and illustrate three things they do to calm themselves.

I Know Anger Gets Ahold of Me When

Use 2.1 C "Anger Gets Ahold of Me" to help children become more conscious of times when anger gets ahold of them. There are four boxes on the reproducible. In them, students will draw and describe what their face, body and voice feel like when they are angry, and how they might shift their goal.

It Bugs Me When _____!

Goal: To help children become conscious of what bugs them and throws them into an "I am" state of upset

Materials

- [ ] *Listen to Your Feelings* CD Songs:
  - "Anger Got Ahold of Me" #1
  - "Sadness Got Ahold of Me" #22
  - "Bye, Bye Buddies" #4
- [ ] Chart paper
- [ ] Angry, Sad, Scared and Calm Feeling Buddies
- [ ] Reproducibles
  - 2.2 A, 2.2 B, 2.2 C, 2.2 D, 2.2 E, 2.2 F, 2.2 G, 2.2 H (optional, older)
  - 2.2 I, 2.2 J, 2.2 K, 2.2 L (optional, younger)
- [ ] *I Am Upset Smock*
- [ ] Chart paper and/or sentence strips
- [ ] Markers
- [ ] *Shubert Rants and Raves* (optional)
- [ ] Instructional DVD

Before You Begin

- Watch the songs for Lesson 2.2 by selecting "Circle Time" then "Songs By Lesson" on your instructional DVD
- Gather materials
- Write the "Anger Got Ahold of You" chant on sentence strips or chart paper
- Print reproducibles

Let's Get Started

 Sing: "Anger Got Ahold of Me" #1

Hold Angry while singing.

We are going to play a game called "It Bugs Me When _____." Explain that when people say, "It bugs me," they often mean they feel mad or angry.

To play this game, we are going to pass around the *I Am Upset Smock*. I will start the game to show you how to play. Place Angry in your lap.

 Buddy Tip: If you have read *Shubert Rants and Raves* to your classroom, show them the book and ask if they remember what bugged Shubert in the book.

It bugs me when... Give an example of something that really bugs you.

And my face looks like this. Demonstrate.

And my voice sounds loud like this. Demonstrate.

Put on the angry *I Am Upset Smock*. Point to the chant on chart paper or sentence strips, and coach all the children in chanting:

Anger got ahold of you. What can you do?

Forget who you are or be a S.T.A.R.!

I'm going to be a S.T.A.R.

As you and the class begin to take a deep breath, take off the angry *I Am Upset Smock* and lay it on the floor next to you.

Angry: What are you going to do with me now? You can't just toss me on the floor.

I am going to keep you calm and safe by my side so you can be you, and I can be the best me ever. Place Angry by your side, take a deep breath and say to Angry, **You're safe. Keep breathing. You can handle this.**

Adaptation for Younger Students: Play the game throughout the day in small groups so each child has a turn. Have the student wearing the smock sit in the middle of a circle to share something that bugs him/her. The students around the circle stand and act bug crazy mad by stomping their feet, clenching their fists and making angry faces. They sit down as they chant, "Anger got ahold of you," then S.T.A.R. together and say, "You're safe. Keep breathing. You can handle this."

Play the game with as many children as possible based on time and interest. Write "It Bugs Me When" across the top of chart paper. Summarize children's triggers on the paper. Save this chart paper for use with Lesson 2.3.

We have been talking a lot about anger, but we have many Feeling Buddies. Point to all the Buddies in their pocket homes.

When we first feel any emotion, we get lost in it, just like we get lost in anger. We feel out of control and sometimes do things that are hurtful to ourselves and others. We are going to learn a new song called "Sadness Got Ahold of Me." (Do the same partner game as when you sang "Anger Got Ahold of Me.")

 Sing: "Sadness Got Ahold of Me" #22

Adaptation for Younger Students: When teaching "Sadness Got Ahold of Me," focus on one verse at a time. You may need to teach the song over multiple days.

Point to the four core Feeling Buddies on the top row of their Feeling Buddies pocket home.

Sometimes anger gets a hold of us. Hold up Angry.

Sometimes sadness gets a hold of us. Hold up Sad.

Sometimes scared gets ahold of us. Hold up Scared.

Sometimes happy gets ahold of us. Hold up Happy.

 Sing: "Bye, Bye Buddies" #4

Commitment: Our commitment this week is to be aware of what bugs us so we can choose to take off the *I Am Upset Smock* to be helpful. Make this commitment with me by turning to a friend and repeating the last line of our chant. Point to the last line of the chant on your chart paper or sentence strips. I'm going to be a S.T.A.R.

Extension Activities

All Ages

Sadness Got Ahold of Me

Play "Sadness Got Ahold of Me." Instruct children to listen, act out the verses and sing along. Afterwards, share a time when sadness got ahold of you. Encourage children who wish to share to tell their stories. Use the sad side of the *I Am Upset Smock* the same way you used the angry side earlier in the lesson.

"Angry's Got Ahold of Me" Tag

1. One person is "it." This person is Angry.
2. One person is the S.T.A.R. Helper.
3. Everyone else runs from Angry.
4. If Angry tags you, you must freeze until the S.T.A.R. Helper comes to S.T.A.R. with you. Then you both are S.T.A.R. Helpers. You hold hands to go breathe with others.
5. Angry can't tag anyone in the S.T.A.R. Helpers group. S.T.A.R. Helpers hold hands so Angry knows who is in this group.
6. The S.T.A.R. Helper group grows larger as they hold hands, unfreeze and breathe with each person Angry has tagged.
7. The game ends naturally when everyone is a S.T.A.R. Helper. Angry can pick a new person to be Angry, and the game begins again.

Finding What Bugs Me

Children will draw and/or write about things that bug them, triggering the feeling pictured on the reproducible. Older children can choose from the feelings in reproducibles 2.2 A, 2.2 B, 2.2 C, 2.2 D, 2.2 E, 2.2 F, 2.2 G and 2.2 H themselves. Younger children will use only reproducibles 2.2 I, 2.2 J, 2.2 K and 2.2 L. Complete as many reproducibles as time allows.

Breathe and Think

Goal: To understand the importance of removing the *I Am Upset Smock* in order to become your usual thinking self, capable of choosing to be helpful instead of hurtful

Materials

- ❑ *Listen to Your Feelings* CD Songs:
  - "Buddy Helper" #3
  - "In My Body" #15
  - "Breathe" #2
- ❑ Reproducibles
  - 2.3 A (optional, younger)
  - 2.3 B, 2.3 C, 2.3 D (optional, older)
- ❑ Angry Feeling Buddy
- ❑ *I Am Upset Smock*
- ❑ Chart paper from Lesson 2.1 (optional)
- ❑ Instructional DVD

Before You Begin

- Watch the songs for Lesson 2.3 by selecting "Circle Time" then "Songs By Lesson" on your instructional DVD
- Gather materials
- Print reproducibles

Let's Get Started

 Sing: "In My Body" #15

Last time we talked about when anger gets ahold of us. Did any of you begin to notice when you could feel anger in your body? What did it feel like? Did anyone notice what anger looked like on someone's face? How your tone of voice or a friend's tone of voice sounded?

 Buddy Tip: It is helpful to say the same sentence in different tones of voice to show how tone carries meaning.

Look what happens when anger gets ahold of you. Put Angry in your lap. Put on the angry *I Am Upset Smock*. Lower your head and look at your feet to show that when the smock is on, your thinking brain turns off.

You can't be helpful and solve the problem when your thinking brain is off. You can only be hurtful. Help me take off my angry smock by being a S.T.A.R. Let's all breathe. Remember, three deep breaths are helpful.

Be a S.T.A.R. and remove the smock. Lift your head up and look around. Put your hand to your chin as if you are thinking about helpful solutions to a problem.

Look, I can start to think again! Have young children use an energy ball or energy stick (available on ConsciousDiscipline.com) to represent the thinking brain turning off and on.

Angry: Glad you helped. My job isn't to help solve problems. My job is to get you to change what you're doing because what you are doing isn't working. Solving problems is your job.

Earlier we acted out verses to the song "Anger Got a Hold of Me." Today, we are going to act out situations where anger got a hold of us. I will go first to show you how we will do it. Then it will be your turn to practice.

Select a current situation from your school life, for example:
A teacher borrowed several books from my classroom without asking. I went to read one of those books for a lesson and it was nowhere to be found, throwing off the morning schedule. I could feel anger begin to get ahold of me. My heart started beating and my face started getting hot.

Tell your story to the children and model the process. Put on the smock and lower your head.

Anger got ahold of me when I was looking for the book the other teacher borrowed without asking. Change your tone.
She knows better than this! Demonstrate anger visuals on face and body.
I should take stuff out of her room and see if she likes it!
But that would be hurtful.
I am going to breathe three times and calm down so I can think of how to be helpful instead of hurtful. Take three breaths slowly and consciously. Take off the smock, raise your head and look around.

I'm back. Whew, I was lost in anger. Now I can think about how to solve the problem. I've got it!
I will talk to her. I will say, "I don't like it when you borrow books without asking. Please return my books and ask me next time before taking anything out of my room."

Now it is time for the children to practice. Use the following process to help them be successful.

1. The child puts on the angry *I Am Upset Smock* and says, "When anger got ahold of me, I _____" and tells the story. Point out that with the smock on, our thinking brain goes offline and we can only come up with hurtful ways to attempt to solve a problem. Instruct the children who are listening to chant, "Anger got ahold of you," on your signal.

2. Then prompt the child to be a S.T.A.R. and take off the angry *I Am Upset Smock* while simultaneously raising his or her head. Point out that with the smock off, we can begin to think and come up with helpful ways to solve our problems. The children who are watching join together to be a S.T.A.R. to help get the smock off.

3. The child can brainstorm helpful instead of hurtful ways to solve the problem. The children listening can help with the brainstorming.

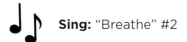 **Sing:** "Breathe" #2

Commitment: Our commitment this week is to ask ourselves and each other, "Am I being helpful or hurtful?" If the answer is hurtful, we will be a S.T.A.R. and think of helpful solutions. If the answer is helpful, we will say to ourselves and others, "You are doing it. You are choosing to be helpful!" If you agree to this commitment, give a friend a high five.

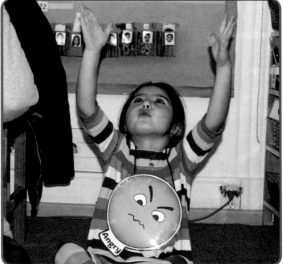

Extension Activities

All Ages

Group Problem Solving

Bring out the chart paper from Lesson 2.2 that lists times the children have felt bugged. Does anyone have something on this list they are still having a hard time thinking of a helpful way to solve? Are you willing to hear what some other children have done? If yes: Who has solved a problem like this and would like to offer help? If no: (Child's name) has chosen to pass. Who would like a turn next?

Younger

From Hurtful Words to Helpful Words

Distribute reproducible 2.3 A "From Hurtful Words to Helpful Words." Have students draw the feeling face that they think goes with the words written in the speech bubble. Print large feeling faces from templates (T.5 Angry, Scared, Sad and Happy). Place on white board with magnets at child's level. Have the speech bubbles prepared with phases that the different Buddies might say. Place magnetic tape on the back of each bubble. Read the phrases and have students take turns placing the bubble over the appropriate Buddy. For example: "I miss my dog." "Go away!" "I can handle this."

Older

What Bugs Me

Students illustrate what bugs them and how to calm down with reproducible 2.3 B "What Bugs Me." First draw a picture and/or write about a time when something bugged you. Then draw a picture and/or write about what you could do differently to calm down enough to be helpful instead of hurtful.

Anger Got Ahold of Me

Using reproducible 2.3 C "Anger Got Ahold of Me," children will draw a picture of themselves when angry. At the bottom, ask them to think of the first words they might say.

From Hurtful Words to Helpful Words

Distribute reproducible 2.3 D "From Hurtful Words to Helpful Words." Have students write words in the speech bubbles to match the feelings pictured beneath.

Going to the Safe Place

Goal: To teach children to go to the Safe Place when a feeling gets ahold of them to give them time and space to remove the *I Am Upset Smock*

Materials

- ❏ *Listen to Your Feelings* CD Song:
  - "Choose to Be a S.T.A.R." #5
- ❏ Angry, Sad, Scared and Calm Feeling Buddies
- ❏ Reproducible
  - 2.4 A (optional, older)
- ❏ Safe Place
- ❏ *I Am Upset Smock*
- ❏ Crepe paper or caution tape
- ❏ Chart paper or sentence strips
- ❏ Instructional DVD

Word Wall

Safe Place, S.T.A.R.

Before You Begin

- Watch "Overview of Safe Place" and "Setting Up Your Safe Place" in the "Safe Place" section of your instructional DVD
- Watch the songs for Lesson 2.4 by selecting "Circle Time" then "Songs By Lesson" on your instructional DVD
- Print reproducibles
- Set up your Safe Place
- Gather materials
- Write the Celebration Chant on chart paper or sentence strips
- Make preparations for putting your Buddies and their pocket home in the Safe Place
- **Word Wall:** Safe Place, S.T.A.R.

Let's Get Started

 Sing: "Choose to Be a S.T.A.R." #5

 Conscious Discipline Tip: Remember, noticing means to describe what you saw without judgment. A noticing statement sounds like this, "Yesterday while walking to the cafeteria, Shanita was getting crowded in the line. Her face began to look like this (demonstrate). Anger got ahold of her. Instead of pushing, she took a deep breath and said, *Move forward Ryan, I'm getting smashed*. She chose to take off her angry *I Am Upset Smock* by being a S.T.A.R. so she could solve her problems."

Many of you are choosing to be a S.T.A.R. when anger gets ahold of you. Notice several situations you have seen in the classroom, halls, lunchroom or playground.

Who can share a time when they were powerful enough to take off their angry *I Am Upset Smock* by choosing to be a S.T.A.R.? Share a personal story of your own if needed to start the sharing process. After each sharing, have the other children celebrate with the following celebration chant. "That was helpful. You helped our class be strong. That was helpful so we all can get along." Point to the words on the chart paper or sentence strips as you chant.

Buddy Tip: Choose a quiet, cozy area in your classroom that will be your Safe Place. If you are implementing Conscious Discipline, you will already have a Safe Place in your classroom. If you are new to Conscious Discipline, setting up the Safe Place is essential before conducting this lesson. The Safe Place is your classroom's self-regulation learning center. It is a physical structure that contains activities and tools that empower children to change their inner states from upset to calm through the five-step process you are teaching in the *Curriculum*. You will be adding tools to the area throughout the year to help children learn to self-regulate emotions and behaviors. The look and feel of the Safe Place is one of warmth, invitation and comfort. A picture and explanation of an ideal Safe Place is on page xiv. Additional helpful resources for creating this learning center can be found in *Creating the School Family*: Chapter 9, *Conscious Discipline*: Chapter 1 and Shubert's Classroom at ConsciousDiscipline.com.

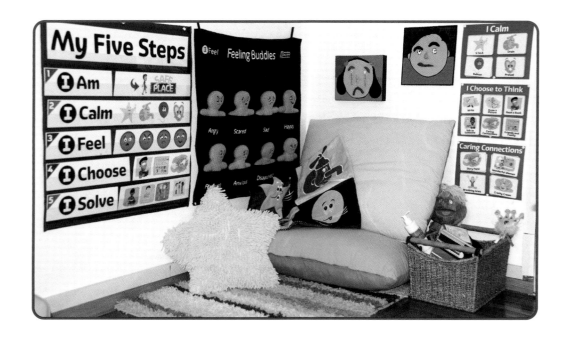

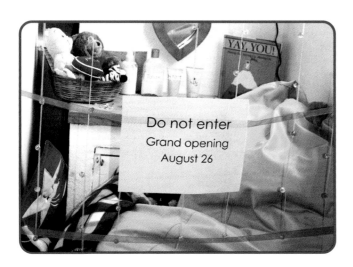

Rope off the Safe Place with crepe paper or caution tape for the ribbon cutting ceremony that is part of this lesson. If you are already using a Safe Place in your classroom, you can have a "Grand Re-Opening Ceremony" or skip this part of the lesson.

Has anyone noticed a new center in our classroom? It's called the Safe Place! I wonder what we might use the Safe Place for? Here is a hint before you start guessing: It will help us all keep the classroom safe and will be the new home for our Feeling Buddies. Have children guess and continue giving hints until excitement dwindles.

Sometimes it's hard to choose to be a S.T.A.R when strong feelings get ahold of us. We might let anger get ahold of us and push, hit or call someone a hurtful name. We might let sadness get ahold of us and find it hard to pay attention in class. This new center is a place we all can go when anger gets ahold of us. Hold up Angry.
Or sadness gets ahold of us. Hold up Sad.
Or scared gets ahold of us. Hold up Scared.
The Safe Place is a place where you can go to take off your *I Am Upset Smock* and turn your thinking brain back on.

We will go to the Safe Place to help change strong feelings to feeling calm by breathing and doing other activities you will find there. I will teach you more about how to help your Feeling Buddies in the Safe Place over the next few weeks.

If you have a Conscious Discipline classroom, you may have already opened the Safe Place. If that is the case, ceremoniously hang the Feeling Buddies in the Safe Place when you are ready to teach "Step 3: I Feel."

I think it's time to open our Safe Place for use. What do you think? Gather the children at the Safe Place, conduct a short opening ceremony, cut the crepe paper or caution tape, and declare the Safe Place open for children to use. Hang up the Feeling Buddies in their pocket home and show the children the My Five Steps pocket chart.

Adaptations for Younger Students: Model and remind students of your Safe Place expectations. What does using the Safe Place look like? What does it sound like? When do you use the Safe Place? Provide times throughout the day for each child to go into the Safe Place to practice being a S.T.A.R.

Hang the pocket chart on the white board with the title "My Five Steps" at the top. Place the rest of the cards in pockets as you introduce each step.

We will be learning five steps. So far, we have learned two of them. Show the "Step 1: I Am" sentence strip and place it in the pocket chart. Show the "Step 2: I Calm" sentence strip and place it in the pocket chart with the S.T.A.R. icon.

You can see there are still some blank spaces! We still have more learning to do with our Feeling Buddies! Point to the blank spaces. You may also want to show a few items from the Safe Place Case. When you are finished, tell children to return to their seats or the circle.

Now we are going to play a game called "Freeze and Move" to practice going to the Safe Place. In this game, I will tell a story and two children will take turns acting it out. When I say, "Freeze," they will freeze. Demonstrate "freezing" by holding perfectly still.

I will ask some questions while they are still frozen. Then we will all say, "Move," and see what happens in response to my questions.

Select children to role-play the following situation:

Two children, X and Y (fill in the children's names) are sitting next to each other on the floor. X is leaning on Y, thinking it is funny. Y says, "Stop it," and X keeps on leaning and laughing. Then anger gets ahold of Y.

At this point, hold up your hand and say, "Freeze." Ask the following questions:

How do you know anger got ahold of Y?
Answers: The face, arms, hands and voice are giving signals Y might be hurtful to X.

Where could Y go if anger got ahold of him or her?
Answer: Safe Place.

What could Y do when he or she gets to the Safe Place?
Answers: Be a S.T.A.R. and calm down.

We are going to count to three and then say, "Move." Then we are going to watch to see how Y chooses to be helpful by going to the Safe Place and calming down.

Celebrate the choice to be helpful. **You did it! You chose to be helpful.** Encourage children to use the Celebration Chant they are learning by pointing to the sentence strips or chart paper where you wrote it.

If the child chooses not to be helpful and instead chooses to hit, set the limit and coach the helpful action. **You seem angry. You wanted X to stay in his (or her) own space and you forgot the words to say. You may not hit. Hitting hurts. When you are angry, go to the Safe Place and choose something to help you calm down. Then you can solve your problem.** Guide the child to the Safe Place and then celebrate. **You did it! You went to the Safe Pace to calm down.**

Adapt and repeat the process for common situations from your classroom.

 Buddy Tip: Consider adding the Safe Place to your center rotation. When it is time to use the Safe Place, younger children will choose to visit the Safe Place and practice strategies. Older children will write in their journals.

 Sing: "Choose to be a S.T.A.R." #5

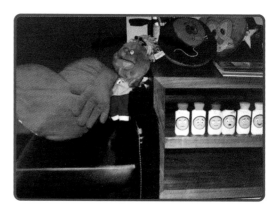

Commitment: Our commitment this week is to take ourselves to the Safe Place and practice changing our inner state from angry to calm by being a S.T.A.R. Hold up Calm. Who is willing to practice? On three, point to your chest with your thumbs and say, "I'm willing. 1-2-3!"

Extension Activities

All Ages

Safe Place Tag
Pick a location outside (like a tree or picnic table) to serve as the Safe Place. Choose one person to be the Star Helper. The Star Helper runs to tag another child and bring him or her to the Safe Place where they will S.T.A.R. together. After they S.T.A.R. together, the Star Helper stays in the Safe Place and the tagged child becomes the new Star Helper. This new Star Helper runs out to tag others and repeat the process. There is always just one person in the Safe Place at a time. The game naturally ends when all students have had a turn being Star Helpers.

Safe Place Class Book
Create a Safe Place class book that shows when you can go to the Safe Place (feelings got ahold of you, not having a good day, missing your mom, etc.), the purpose of the Safe Place (to practice managing our feelings so we can solve problems in a helpful way) and the Safe Place guidelines (how long can you stay, how many people at a time, etc.).

Older

Observational Drawing
Have the children complete an observational drawing of the class Safe Place, paying close attention to each item in it and using reproducible 2.4 A "Draw Our Safe Place" as a frame.

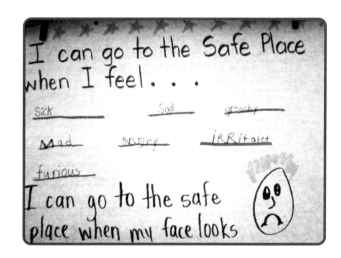

The "It Bugs Me When" Class Book

Goal: To become more conscious of people and situations that trigger our intense anger

Materials

- *Listen to Your Feelings* CD (Choose songs from previous lessons)
- Angry Feeling Buddy
- Reproducibles
  - 2.5 A, 2.5 B, 2.5 C, 2.5 D (all ages)
- "It Bugs Me When" chart paper from Lesson 2.2
- Bug Crazy Mad Shubert picture
- Pencils, markers and crayons
- Camera
- Instructional DVD

Before You Begin

- Watch the instructional DVD to choose songs to use in this lesson by selecting "Circle Time" then "Songs By Lesson"
- Gather materials
- Print reproducibles

Let's Get Started

 Sing: Choose a song from the previous lesson

Our commitment last time was to go to the Safe Place. Notice several situations like, "Jay had a hard morning so he went to the Safe Place and took three deep breaths (demonstrate)."

 Conscious Discipline Tip: When noticing, remember to begin with "you" or the child's name, not "I noticed." Be careful not to judge the situation with phrases like, "I like the way you went to the Safe Place," and "Good job using the Safe Place." Also, never use tangible rewards for children who choose to use the Safe Place. Self-regulation requires a willingness that comes from within a person. Judgment and rewards (giving stickers, etc.) are external motivators, and will impede this very important developmental journey for children.

Some of you went to the Safe Place when something bugged you. Who remembers when we played the "It Bugs Me When" game? I wrote your answers on this chart paper. Review some of the answers and repeat the game, eliciting additional insights from children as they continue to identify people and situations that trigger intense anger within them.

Who has additional "bug me" moments to add to our list? We are going play "It Bugs Me When" again, listing all the ways people and situations bug us. I will add them to our chart paper. Pass around the "It Bugs Me When" Shubert picture. Prompt children to respond by saying, "It Bugs Me When" and record their answers on the chart paper.

 Adaptations for Younger Students: Instead of adding to the "It Bugs Me" list, review answers already on the chart. Have students act out the scenarios using the same format as you did in Lesson 2.2.

Now we're going to do a writing activity about things that really, really bug us. Look at the chart paper and choose one thing that really, really bugs you. You are going to draw or write about a time when you were really, really bugged.

Hold up the reproducible that is best for your age group, 2.5 A, 2.5 B or 2.5 C "When Do You Feel Bug Crazy." Let younger children know they will have an opportunity to tell a teacher what to write to on their papers to go with their drawings.

As you work, I am going to come around and take a photo of you making an angry face. At the end, I am going to put all the pages and photos together in a class book.

 Adaptations for Younger Students: Ahead of time, prepare each child's page by writing down the trigger from the class chart. The children will then illustrate that situation.

Distribute the reproducibles with pencils, crayons and/or markers. Repeat the instructions as needed for them to be successful.

1. Look at the chart paper and choose one situation that really, really bugs you.
2. Write that situation in the blank on the top of your paper.
3. Illustrate a situation like that from your own life.

As the children are working, walk around and take a photo of each child holding the angry Feeling Buddy and making an angry face. Collect the children's pages, glue their photos to their pages and bind all the pages together. Print and attach the cover for the book, reproducible 2.5 D "Our Bug Crazy Book."

Sing: Choose a song from the previous lesson

Commitment: Our commitment this week is to choose to be a S.T.A.R. or take ourselves to the Safe Place when we feel really, really bugged. Point to the Safe Place three times if you agree to this commitment. 1-2-3!

It bugs me when Cody, my brother, doesn't let me in his room. It bugs me when he turns up his radio too loud. I say "Stop, it! I don't like it when it's up like that." He says "I don't care". Then I tell on him and my Mom says "Turn it off" and then Cody is grounded to his room. It makes me feel good.

When I'm in a hurry and I get stuck in traffic, it really bugs me. When I have to exchange something at _____, it bugs me to have to stand in line for a l---o---n----g time. It bugs me when I put toothpaste on my toothbrush and it falls off into the sink. Yuck!

Resources

Managing Emotional Mayhem
- Chapter 5: The Child's Journey: Coaching Children in the Five-Step Process

Creating the School Family
- Chapter 9: The Safe Place

Conscious Discipline: Building Resilient Classrooms
- Chapter 1: Composure

Shubert's School on ConsciousDiscipline.com/Shubert
- Click on the Safe Place to see images and video of classroom Safe Places

School Family Job Set
- Provide you the structure and information to give a job for every class member.

Shubert is a S.T.A.R.

Shubert Rants and Raves

Brain Smart Choices for Connection and Calming

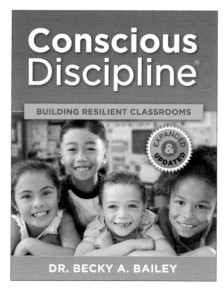

Conscious Discipline

Shubert Rants and Raves

Progress Check

Check your children's progress. Can your children:

1. Tell you at least two things that "bug" them?

2. Tell you what they can do to take off the *I Am Upset Smock*?

3. Go to the Safe Place when anger gets ahold of them?

3

I Calm Myself

Strong Emotions

Goal: To recognize what strong emotions feel like in our bodies and understand what happens in our brains

Materials

- *Listen to Your Feelings* CD
  Songs:
  - "In My Body" #15
  - "Solutions" #23
- Angry and Scared Feeling Buddies
- Reproducibles
  - 3.1 A, 3.1 B (optional, all ages)
- Feelings Bottle (one full, one empty)
- *Managing Emotional Mayhem*
- Instructional DVD
- Chart paper or sentence strips

Word Wall

Rant, Rave, Respiration

Before You Begin

- Watch the "Step 2: I Calm" video in the "Safe Place" section on your instructional DVD
- Watch the songs for Lesson 3.1 by selecting "Circle Time" then "Songs By Lesson" on your instructional DVD
- Review *Managing Emotional Mayhem*, Chapter 5
- Gather materials (Create the Feelings Bottle by adding food coloring to water. Seal tightly.)
- Print reproducibles
- Write the chant on sentence strips or chart paper and draw a simple picture for each motion in the chant
- **Word Wall:** Rant, Rave, Respiration

Let's Get Started

 Sing: "In My Body" #15

Today we are going to talk about how strong emotions feel in our bodies. An example of a strong emotion would be when we are really, really angry.

Who remembers a time when they were really, really angry, like this much... Hold your arms open wide, showing a large space. Who wants to share what happened?

Hold up Angry. **What do you think your face looks like when you feel really, really angry? Show me.**
What do you think your hands look like?
What do you think your arms look like?
What do you think your whole body looks like?
What do you think your voice sounds like?

Angry: Wow! You all look just like me! Do you remember what I like to say? I'll rant and I'll rave. Something's bugging me! Nothing will change until I breathe.

That's right, Angry. Now lets all be a S.T.A.R. and relax our bodies so we can think better as we listen to this next question carefully: What does this strong emotion (hold your arms out wide again) feel like in your body?

Show the children the Feelings Bottle. It's sometimes hard to explain what it feels like inside our body. Strong emotions might feel like this inside our bodies. Shake the bottle. When we have a strong emotion, three things happen:

1. We hold our breath. Demonstrate by holding your breath.
2. We turn off our thinking brain. Put your head down.
3. We cannot solve our problems. Cover your eyes with your hands.

Adaptations for Older Students: For older children, relate what happens in the body to a science lesson about heart rate and respiration.

Make this into a chant with motions to help the children remember what happens.
Strong emotion. Hold hands out wide.
I hold my breath. Suck in air and hold it.
I can't think. Put your head down.
Solutions I cannot find. Cover your eyes with your hands.

Who remembers a time when they were really, really scared like this much? Hold your arms open wide, showing a large space. Who wants to tell us what happened? Reflect and summarize children's sharing.

Conscious Discipline Tip: Reflecting what children say back to them helps them better understand their own experiences. Your goal is to validate and clarify without adding judgment. Start your reflection with, "So you _____," and then summarize. "So you felt really, really angry when your brother kicked you. You wanted to hit him hard and get him in trouble with your mom." "So you felt really sad when your dog got hit by a car. You threw yourself on the bed, cried and pulled on your teddy bear's fur. You wanted to cry and cry until Fido came home from the vet hospital."

What do you think your face looks like when you feel really, really scared? Show me.
What do you think your hands look like?
What do you think your arms look like?
What do you think your whole body looks like? Stand up and show me.
What do you think your voice sounds like?

Scared: Wow! You all look just like me! Do you remember what I like to say? Oh my, fear, fear, fear. Seek safety, there's a Safekeeper near!

I remember that, Scared. Now, lets all be a S.T.A.R., relax our bodies so we can think better, and listen to this next question carefully: **What does this strong emotion** (hold your arms out wide again) **feel like in your body?**

Show the children the Feelings Bottle again. **When we have a strong emotions three things happen.** Repeat the chant with the motions.
Strong emotion. Hold hands out wide.
I hold my breath. Suck in air and hold it.
I can't think. Put your head down.
Solutions I cannot find. Cover your eyes with your hands.

Continue this process with as many emotions as you have time for or that seem appropriate for your particular age and group of children. Do not shake the bottle at all for calm. Use an empty bottle for sad and say that when we feel really sad, we feel empty inside like all the love is gone. That's why we have friends to help us fill our hearts with love and kindness.

Our job with strong emotions (hold your arms out wide) **is to calm down.** Move your hands together to about half the distance. **One way we have learned to do this is by being a S.T.A.R.**

 Sing: "Solutions" #23

Buddy Tip: Once you have introduced this song, play it at various times, for transitions or "Brain Breaks" because it reminds children what to do when a strong emotion comes so solutions can be found.

Commitment: Our commitment this week is to feel our strong emotions inside us, choose to S.T.A.R. and calm down so we can solve our problems. Give a friend a high five to make this commitment.

Extension Activities

All Ages

Calm versus Angry: Use reproducible 3.1 A "Calm vs. Angry." Have children color the bottles to represent the feeling states.

In My Body: Revisit the part of the lesson where you discussed how a strong feeling feels in your body. Now ask children to color the Feeling Buddy outline in reproducible 3.1 B "In My Body" to show where they feel strong emotions. You may wish to show a sample and describe what you drew to help children get started.

Younger

Breathing Practice: Give students many different opportunities to practice breathing. Have students imagine they are "smelling a flower, then blowing out a candle." During outside time, distribute bubbles or pinwheels for children to use for breathing practice.

Older

Respiration Test: Challenge students to record their respiration for one minute (the number of breaths they take) and their heart rate. As they finish, announce that the principal is coming to their classroom to administer a big test this afternoon, and you are concerned because the other teachers say the test is really hard. Ask students to retake their heart rate and respiration. After recording the results, tell them the test isn't real and discuss the outcomes of the activity. Did their respiration and heart rates change? What does fear do to breathing and heart rate?

Belly Breathing

Goal: To learn S.T.A.R. belly breathing so all children can access the relaxation response in their bodies

Materials

- ☐ *Listen to Your Feelings* CD
  Songs:
  - "Breathe" #2
  - "Choose to Be a S.T.A.R." #5
- ☐ All the Feeling Buddies
- ☐ Reproducible
  - 3.2 A (optional)
- ☐ My Five Steps pocket chart and sentence strips for Steps 1 - 2
- ☐ Feelings Bottle
- ☐ S.T.A.R. icon, *Safe Place Mat* or star wand
- ☐ *I Am Upset Smock*
- ☐ A stuffed animal, Feeling Buddy, small book or object for every child
- ☐ Popsicle sticks, glitter, ribbon, star cutouts, etc. (optional, younger classrooms)
- ☐ Instructional DVD

Word Wall

Shallow, Inhale

Before You Begin

- Watch the songs for Lesson 3.2 by selecting "Circle Time" then "Songs By Lesson" on your instructional DVD
- Review *Managing Emotional Mayhem*, Chapter 5
- Gather materials
- **Word Wall:** Shallow, Inhale

Let's Get Started

 Sing: "Breathe" #2

For the past few weeks we have been practicing becoming aware of what bugs us and what happens when our feelings gets ahold of us. Next, we are going to learn about the different steps we can take to calm down.

When a feeling gets ahold of you, your first step is to go to the Safe Place. Hold up the corresponding sentence strip from the My Five Steps pocket chart.

Instead of being hurtful with our emotions, we have been choosing to be helpful by going to the Safe Place and being a S.T.A.R. Who has been to the Safe Place? Has anyone found this strategy helpful?

After children share their successes, sum up their experiences and repeat them back to the class. An example of a summary statement is, "So you felt yourself getting angry, heard your voice change and noticed how your body felt. You decided to walk to the Safe Place and took a breath instead of pushing Louis back. Good for you. You did it."

Step 2 is to choose a way to calm down. Hold up the corresponding sentence strip from the My Five Steps pocket chart.

We started our Feeling Buddy time together with the song "Breathe." Breathing helps us take off our *I Am Upset Smock*, find ourselves, calm down and start our helpful thinking.

Hold up the Feelings Bottle. When someone bugs us, our insides get like this. Shake the bottle. **Our feelings get ahold of us. Today we will learn more about being a S.T.A.R. We are going to learn how to belly breathe so when we are upset our insides can go from this...** Shake the bottle. **To this...** Stop shaking the bottle. **And from angry to calm.** Hold up the Feeling Buddies Angry and Calm.

See if you can feel the difference between being a S.T.A.R. using slow conscious belly breathing and taking short, fast, shallow breaths like a bull ready to charge. Have the children be a S.T.A.R. and then pretend to be a bull, quickly snorting air in and out. After each breathing exercise, ask children to shut their eyes and pay attention to how their bodies feel.

Can you feel the difference between being a S.T.A.R. using deep breathing to make your belly move, and pretending to be a bull breathing shallow and fast?

Everyone put your hands on your bellies. Demonstrate for the children how to lightly place both hands on their bellies, close to their belly buttons, with the fingertips of each hand slightly touching in the middle of their tummies.

 **Very Important Buddy Tip:** S.T.A.R. breathing is a form of belly breathing scientifically known as diaphragmatic breathing. 70 percent of our metabolic waste is released from the body through breathing. The remaining toxins are released through perspiration, urination and defecation. So, if we believe going to the bathroom is important, then breathing properly must also be at the top of our health list! Extensive research indicates the best predictor of life expectancy is our breathing capacity. Consciously breathing by being a S.T.A.R. releases toxins from the body, improves the immune system, balances the nervous system, turns off the stress response, facilitates weight loss, helps release unhealthy memories and stifled emotions, and integrates our brain to engage the higher centers for optimal functioning. Being a S.T.A.R. is not a technique to "get children quiet," but a strategy for healing, balance, well-being and problem solving.

Now we are going to take in air through our nose. This is called "inhaling."
We inhale and have our bellies go out.
See how our bellies get bigger and it pulls our fingers apart?
Then we let the air out slowly through our mouths and have our bellies pull in.
See how our bellies get smaller and our fingers come back together?

Demonstrate this a few times and observe who is getting it and who is still having trouble. Children who live in chronic stress environments will need more practice and coaching. Repeat the process several times.

Breathe in through your nose and have your belly go out, filling with air. Exhale slowly through your mouth and have your belly go in, letting air out.

Angry: I'm glad we are all going to practice being a S.T.A.R. because I need a lot of help calming down at times. You might have to be a S.T.A.R. many times or go to the Safe Place so you have more time to calm. When your insides feel like this (have Anger shake the Feelings Bottle), I've got ahold of you and you can't think.

Insert the Buddy Helper to give each child a stuffed animal, Feeling Buddy, small book or object to use for the next activity. Have the children sit on the floor in a circle and rotate their bodies so their backs face the inside of the circle. Then have them lay down carefully with their heads toward the center of the circle and their legs facing out. Check to see that everyone is in position before beginning. (Do this activity as a whole group as part of this lesson. Repeat the activity many times if you teach children ages six and younger. They require multiple experiences to feel what belly breathing is like.)

Now, put your object on your tummy.

When you take a deep breath in through your nose, notice how your object goes up.

When you let the air out, the object goes down!

Let's practice. See if you can make your object go up and down as you breathe deeply.

Remember to hold your body still and move the object with just your breathing.

That's it! You're doing it.

Notice several children who are being successful or trying. You might say, "Kareem took a deep breath and his belly was so big that he had to reposition his book. It was tumbling off his belly! Casey's bear was not moving, but she kept trying and now it's beginning to move with her breathing." If children have trouble, place one object on their chests and another object on their bellies. Have them practice breathing so the objects on their chests stay still and the objects on their bellies move.

Now we are going to add something else. I am going to count to four as you breathe in slowly through your nose, having your belly rise. Then I am going to count to eight as you exhale slowly with your belly going down. Demonstrate this several times so everyone understands the task.

Place your object on your belly, hands by your side.

Inhale air through your nose slowly. 1-2-3-4.

Now exhale. 1-2-slowly-3-4-5-6-7-8.

You did it! You inhaled through your nose like you were smelling a flower and you exhaled slowly like you were blowing up a great, big balloon.

Good for you!

Adaptations for Younger Students: If your students take a nap, give each child a small plush star or animal to use to practice belly breathing as they prepare to sleep.

Observe and coach those having difficulty. Problems to look for:

- Belly does not move
- Shoulders/chest move up and down
- Fast breaths
  (For children who are having difficulty, do this activity as a small group activity.)

Have the children sit up and return to facing each other in the circle. The Buddy Helper collects the objects used in the exercise.

Introduce the class signal for being a S.T.A.R. Your signal could be holding up the *Safe Place Mat*, a printout of the S.T.A.R. icon, a star wand or similar item.

Now we will sing the song "Breathe" again. Check yourself as you sing to see if your belly goes in and out when you breathe.

 Buddy Tip: This lesson can be extended to a science lesson by discussing the lungs, windpipe and diaphragm. If you choose to extend the lesson, make sure you let the children know that belly breathing is what moves the diaphragm up and down to push the air in and out of the lungs.

 Sing: "Breathe" #2

After singing, have the children look at all the Feeling Buddies and decide which Buddy represents how they are feeling right now. Hopefully they will choose Calm or Happy. Reiterate that feeling calm or happy helps us think better, solve problems better and be better friends to each other.

Commitment: What do you think our commitment this week could be?

Get children's input into creating a commitment from the lesson. Hint: It should be about belly breathing. Summarize the commitment in writing and place it in a central location in the classroom to remind children about it throughout the week.

 Buddy Tip: It is essential to include visual icons of the strategies you expect students to use in the Safe Place for two reasons:

1. The right hemisphere of the brain is in charge of self-regulation and this hemisphere is governed by images.
2. Children govern their behavior with internal images rather than words. The My Five Steps pocket chart and I Choose to Think posters in this kit help children be successful by providing visual images of what to do.

Extension Activities

All Ages

Breathing Steps
During whole group instruction create an anchor chart together. List the steps and add visuals by drawing. Then refer to the anchor chart frequently as you practice belly breathing (four-year-olds). This can also be done for all ages.

Have children draw the belly breathing steps with reproducible 3.2 A "Breathing Steps." For younger children (five to six-year-olds), you may wish to print the four steps in the space provided before you make photocopies. Older children can write the steps themselves.

Step 1: Inhale through the nose
Step 2: The belly goes out
Step 3: Exhale through the mouth
Step 4: The belly goes in

Star Wands
Students make their own breathing star wands. First, trace and cut out a star on card stock or other heavy weight paper. Then tape it to a popsicle stick. Glue on long pieces of ribbon. Decorate with markers, crayons and/or glitter.

Older

Changing the Chant
Review the chant about strong emotions from Lesson 3.1 and lead a discussion. How would this chant change after being a S.T.A.R. by taking some deep belly breaths?

I hold my breath
I can't think
And solutions I cannot find!

Draining and Ballooning

Goal: To learn two more calming self-regulatory strategies

Materials

- *Listen to Your Feelings* CD
  Songs:
  - "I Have Made Some New Friends" #13
  - "Bye, Bye Buddies" #4
- Basket of Buddies
- Feelings Bottle
- S.T.A.R., Drain and Balloon icons
- *Shubert is a S.T.A.R.*
- Instructional DVD
- *Safe Place Mat* (optional)
- Chart paper and markers (optional)
- Reproducibles
  - 3.3 A (optional, younger)
  - 3.3 B (optional, older)

Before You Begin

- Watch the songs for Lesson 3.3 by selecting "Circle Time" then "Songs By Lesson" on your instructional DVD
- Gather materials
- Read *Shubert is a S.T.A.R.*
- Print reproducibles

Buddy Tip: If you are using Conscious Discipline in your classroom, you may have already taught the relaxation techniques (S.T.A.R., Drain, Balloon, Pretzel). We suggest you do Lessons 3.2 and 3.3 as a review and to help children practice. The icons for these relaxation techniques can be downloaded from the Conscious Discipline website under Resources.

Let's Get Started

 Sing: "I Have Made Some New Friends" #13

Prepare by putting the Feeling Buddies in the same order as in the song: Angry, Sad, Disappointed, Anxious, Calm, Scared (If you have only introduced the first four Buddies, sing this song without the CD. The tune is "I've Been Working on the Railroad." Listen to the song to help you learn the rhythm.), Happy then Frustrated. Coach the Buddy Helper to hold up each Feeling Buddy as it is named in the song. Alternately, you could pass out the printable Feeling Buddy faces so each child has one. As you sing have the children with the corresponding Buddy stand up. Then trade with a friend and sing again. This is a great review to identify the faces.

Did you remember the names of all of our Feeling Buddies? Let's see if you can remember their names without singing the song. Have the Feeling Buddy Helper hold up the Feeling Buddies in random order as the children call out their names.

Good for you! You did it. You were able to name all of our Feeling Buddies.
When any feeling gets ahold of us (shake the bottle) **we act out our emotions.**
We might hit if we are angry.
We might hide and run away if we are scared.
We might pout and whine if we are disappointed.
We might throw things if we are frustrated.
Breathing helps our insides calm down. Stop shaking the bottle.
The feeling does not go away. Point out how the water is still a color.
The color does not change, but we find we can manage the feeling. We get to be the boss of our feelings instead of them being the boss of us. We get to say to our Feeling Buddies, "You are safe. I've got ahold of you."

Have the Buddy Helper hold up Angry while the class practices taking three deep breaths and then chants, "You are safe. I've got ahold of you." Repeat this with several Buddies.

As I read this book, *Shubert is a S.T.A.R.,* **see if you notice anything in the book that we use in our classroom.** Read *Shubert is a S.T.A.R.* and learn about a day when Shubert's feelings got ahold of him. Focus on the new breathing strategies of Ballooning and Draining, and pause to give children time to practice these techniques as you read.
At the end of the book, Shubert got ahold of his anger. So can you! Hold up Angry.
Let's practice Draining like Crenshaw and Ballooning like Lucinda one more time. Lead the children in Draining and Ballooning. Then hold up Angry and invite children to repeat after you: **You are safe. I've got ahold of you.**

Angry: Whew. That's better. Thanks, boys and girls. Draining and Ballooning always seem to help me become oozy doozy caterpillar calm! It's helpful when you breathe and say, "You're safe. I've got ahold of you." Put Angry in your lap.

 Adaptations for Younger Students: Blow up a real balloon, then let it go to demonstrate how air fills the balloon and is released, just like when we exhale.

I am going to add Draining and Ballooning to our choices in the Safe Place. Add the Drain and Balloon icons to Step 2 next to the S.T.A.R. icon. Point to the steps on the chart.

Let's review quickly:
So far the process is to go to the Safe Place and choose a Feeling Buddy from its pocket.
Hold the Buddy while you S.T.A.R., Drain or Balloon.
Then tell your Buddy, "You are safe. I've got ahold of you."

 Sing: "Bye, Bye Buddies" #4

Commitment: Our commitment for this week is to Drain, Balloon or be a
S.T.A.R. when our feelings get ahold of us. You can go to the Safe Place to practice
with a Feeling Buddy. Remember to tell your Feeling Buddy, "You're safe. I've got
ahold of you." If you agree to do this, give a thumbs up.

Extension Activities

All Ages

Shubert is a S.T.A.R.
Lead students in completing the appropriate *Shubert is a S.T.A.R.* worksheet for your age group, reproducible 3.3 A (younger) or 3.3 B (older).

Older

Chart It
Use chart paper to create a Venn diagram or thinking map that shows the similarities and differences between your classroom and Shubert's.

The Pretzel

Goal: To learn how to relax the nervous system and return to a calm state through the use of an integrative action called the Pretzel

Materials

- ❏ *Listen to Your Feelings* CD Song:
  - "When I Feel Scared" #27
- ❏ Scared, Angry and Calm Feeling Buddies
- ❏ Reproducible
  - 3.4 A (optional, older)
- ❏ Templates
  - T.2 "Calming Book"
  - T.3 "Portable Safe Place"
- ❏ S.T.A.R., Drain, Balloon and Pretzel icons or the *Safe Place Mat*
- ❏ Feelings Bottle
- ❏ Instructional DVD
- ❏ *Brain Smart Choice Cubes* (optional)
- ❏ Yarn (optional)

Before You Begin

- Watch the songs for Lesson 3.4 by selecting "Circle Time" then "Songs By Lesson" on your instructional DVD
- Print reproducibles
- Practice being a Pretzel until it feels natural
- Print and bind the Calming Book using Template T.2
- Copy, cut out and laminate several copies of Template T.3. Hole punch a corner and tie each set together with yarn to make portable Safe Place breathing reminders to bring along when you leave the room or to send home.

Let's Get Started

 Sing: "When I Feel Scared" #27

Our commitment last time was to continue to calm ourselves by being a S.T.A.R., and using Balloon and Drain. Many of you have been practicing and some of you have also been using the Feeling Buddies.

Notice a few situations you have seen. Remember to use noticing language instead of judgment language. For example, "Some of you came up and removed specific Buddies from their pocket homes to help you practice. I heard several of you holding the Buddy that represented how you were feeling and saying, *You are safe. I've got ahold of you.* You calmed yourself as you calmed your Buddy and then you were able to think, like in the song we just sang."

We can't think when we're really, really scared. We just want to run for safety.

Scared: Yeah. Sometimes that's what needs to happen, like when you are playing outside and it starts lightning and thundering. I show up and you jump really high because you're scared, and then you run inside the house for safety!

But sometimes, we need to calm down enough to think. That's when I need you to help me breathe, breathe, breathe. Lead the class in three deep breaths. Put Scared in your lap.

That's right. We can't think when we're feeling strong feelings. In the song, what did the child do to calm down and relax enough to think? What was the child in the song able to think to do after calming down?

 **Buddy Tip:** The Pretzel is a calming exercise that helps children de-stress and focus. It is a Brain Gym® activity. You can learn more at BrainGym.org. This movement relaxes the central nervous system, connects the electrical circuitry of the body, crosses the center midline to activate both left and right hemispheres of the brain, and helps us become emotionally centered and grounded. You can do the Pretzel sitting or standing.

Today we are going to learn one more calming strategy. It is called the Pretzel. Show the children the icon for the Pretzel. It is called a Pretzel because we are going to twist and cross our bodies.

Demonstrate the Pretzel. Coach children through the steps necessary for putting their bodies in the proper position:

Stand or sit.
Cross your right ankle over your left ankle.
Put your arms out in front of you.
Cross your right wrist over your left.
Turn your hands so your thumbs are pointing down.
Put your palms together and interlace your fingers.
Bend your elbows out, gently turning hands down, towards your body until they rest on the center of your chest.
Put your tongue on the roof of your mouth.
Relax and breathe in this position.

 Buddy Tip: When doing a Pretzel, place your tongue on the roof of your mouth. This connects emotion (limbic system) with reason (prefrontal lobes), providing a more integrative brain state from which to learn and respond to life events.

Adaptations for Younger Students: You can conduct a Pretzel from a sitting position with this song, sung to the tune of "I'm a Little Teapot."

I can be a Pretzel, arms and legs out. Have the children extend their arms and legs straight out from their body.
Cross them over and watch me pout. Have the children cross one leg over the other and one arm over the other.
When I get real angry, a Pretzel I'll be. Hold the position.
Squeeze together, 1–2–3. Have the children squeeze their knees up to their chests, staying in the crossed position. Tell them to inhale deeply and then exhale slowly, placing their tongue on the roof of their mouth.

Now we have learned four ways to change our insides from upset (shake the Feelings Bottle and hold up Angry) **to calm.** Stop shaking the bottle and hold up Calm.

Who can name one of the ways we can calm ourselves and then lead the class in doing it? Continue until the class has demonstrated all four ways. Add the Pretzel icon to Step 2 on the My Five Step pocket chart.

I will provide pictures of all these ways to calm down in the Safe Place. I will post them on the wall, print them in a book (hold up the Calming Book you made from Template T.2) **and bring them with us when we leave the room.** Hold up a portable Safe Place you made from Template T.3.

Let's practice. Review all four breathing activities as a class, pointing to the icons. Put the book in the Safe Place for children to reference.

When a feeling gets ahold of you in our School Family, you are going to calm yourself right away by choosing to be a S.T.A.R., Drain, Balloon or Pretzel, or you will go to the Safe Place if you need more time to calm down.

In the Safe Place, the first thing you will do is to choose one of these four strategies to do (hold up the icons) **to begin to relax your body.**

 Sing: "When I Feel Scared" #27

Commitment: Our School Family commitment this week is to choose to calm down immediately or go to the Safe Place. If you are willing to commit to this, practice being a Pretzel. Good for you! We are working together to make our School Family safer for everyone.

Extension Activities

All Ages

Rock and Roll

If you purchased the *Brain Smart Choices for Connection and Calming*, insert the S.T.A.R., Drain, Balloon and Pretzel icons into four of the pockets on the cube. Leave the other two pockets empty. One child holds the cube with both hands and shakes it. Everyone says, "Rock and roll," and the child holding the cube gently rolls it on the floor. The class will practice the calming activity that lands facing up once the cube stops rolling. If the cube lands with a blank space facing up, the child who rolled it chooses the calming strategy to practice.

Older

Pretzel Steps

Use reproducible 3.4 A "Pretzel Steps" to have the children practice transition words while reviewing the steps for being a Pretzel. Encourage them to take their papers home to teach family members this helpful calming technique.

The "I Calm Myself" Book

Goal: To help children further identify emotional triggers and ways to regain composure by creating a class book

Materials

- *Listen to Your Feelings* CD
  Songs:
  - "Do You Know" #6
  - "Yes, I Can" #29
- Reproducibles
  - 3.5 A, 3.5 B, 3.5 C
    (optional, all ages)
  - 3.5 D, 3.5 E, 3.5 F
    (optional, older)
- Markers or crayons
- Camera (optional)
- Instructional DVD

Before You Begin

- Watch the songs for Lesson 3.5 by selecting "Circle Time" then "Songs By Lesson" on your instructional DVD
- Gather materials
- Print reproducibles
- *I Can Calm* book (optional, available for additional purchase at ConsciousDiscipline.com)

Let's Get Started

 Sing: "Do You Know" #6

We have been practicing ways to know when something bugs us or when a feeling gets ahold of us. Today we are going to write a book about what we have learned. Each of you will select a feeling page to complete for the book. You may pick a page about any feeling. Hold up their choices.

Some of you might want to choose anger. Some of you will choose scared. Continue naming feelings and holding up pages until you have shown all the choices.

Once you choose your feeling, complete the sentence describing when that feeling got ahold of you. Then draw four ways you can calm down.

Give children the reproducible for the feeling they choose, plus supplies to illustrate it. You may need to provide examples like, "I feel angry when my brother bosses me around. I can S.T.A.R., read a book, go to the Safe Place or Pretzel." Or "I feel scared when I go to the doctor. I can S.T.A.R., Balloon, Drain or hug Mommy."

 Buddy Tip: For young children, use only the core emotions (3.5 A "I Feel Angry," 3.5 B "I Feel Sad" and 3.5 C "I Feel Scared"). For older children, include their cousins (3.5 D "I Feel Frustrated," 3.5 E "I Feel Disappointed" and 3.5 F "I Feel Anxious").

When the activity is complete, invite children to share their book page. **Those of you who are willing can share your book page with the class. I'll start by sharing my page.**

For example, "I chose sad. I feel sad sometimes after my son leaves for college because I miss him. When I feel sad, I can S.T.A.R., talk on the phone with a friend, listen to relaxing music or Pretzel." Invite children to share one at a time and read the page they created. Children who do not want to share can choose to pass. Create a cheer to celebrate each person's contribution to the class book. For example, "Hooray, hooray! You got ahold of your feeling today!" If you have a Shubert puppet, have Shubert lead the cheer.

 Conscious Discipline Tip: The Celebration Center is a Conscious Discipline structure designed to honor children's many varied accomplishments. School Family Celebrations often incorporate a special chair, props and a chant—similar to the sharing you are conducting in this lesson! They celebrate many things, from learning a new skateboarding trick to earning an A on a math test to the birth of a sibling. To learn more about the Celebration Center, explore *Creating the School Family*, Chapter 13.

At the end of the activity, bind the pages together and create a class book to keep in the Safe Place or class library.

 Sing: "Yes, I Can" #29

Commitment: I am going to choose to S.T.A.R., Drain, Balloon or Pretzel when I have an upsetting feeling. I have several choices and I can handle it! To make this commitment, say, "I can handle it!" on the count of three. 1-2-3!

Extension Activities

All Ages

Breathe Deeply

Take pictures of each child doing his/her favorite breathing technique in the Safe Place. Post the photos next to the Safe Place or add them to a class book for the Safe Place.

We have a Safe Place. You go there when you are sad or angry. We calm down in the safe place.

Resources

Managing Emotional Mayhem
- Chapter 5: The Child's Journey: Coaching Children in the Five-Step Process

Creating the School Family
- Chapter 9: The Safe Place

Shubert's School on ConsciousDiscipline.com/Shubert
- Click on the Safe Place to see images and video of classroom Safe Places

Shubert is a S.T.A.R.

Brain Smart Choices for Connection and Calming

Safe Place Mat

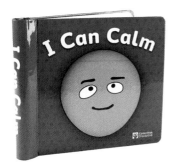

Safe Place Mat

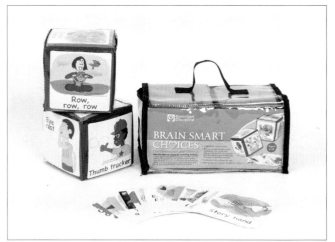

Brain Smart Choices for Connection and Calming

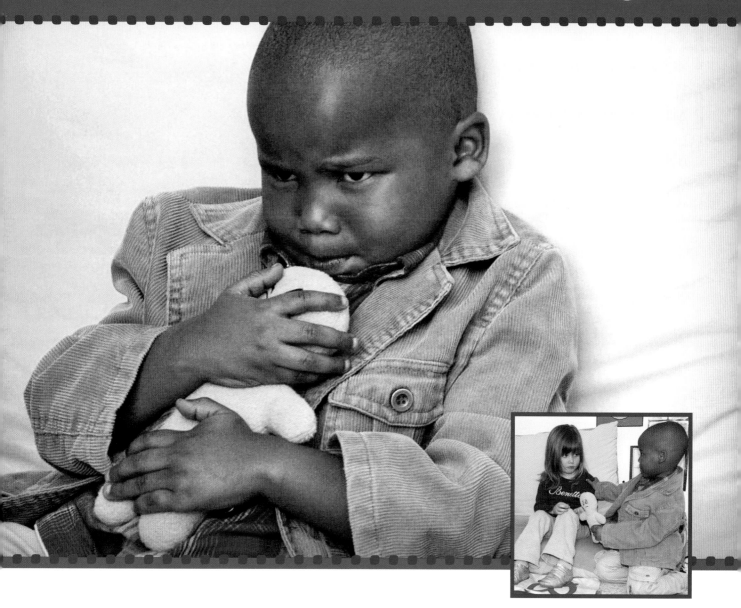

I Feel

Keeping Our Feeling Buddies Safe

Goal: To recognize feeling faces, name the feeling and learn self-regulatory self-talk

Materials

- ❏ *Listen to Your Feelings* CD Songs:
  - "Helping My Buddy" #10
  - "Bye, Bye Buddies" #4
- ❏ Four breathing strategy icons
- ❏ *I Love You Rituals:* ("Row, Row, Row Your Boat")
- ❏ All Buddies from their pocket home and the Buddy basket
- ❏ My Five Steps pocket chart and sentence strips for Steps 1-3
- ❏ Template
  - T.4 "Buddy Bodies" (optional)
- ❏ Feeling Face stickers (optional)
- ❏ Instructional DVD
- ❏ *Managing Emotional Mayhem*

Word Wall

Merrily

Before You Begin

- Review *Managing Emotional Mayhem*, Chapter 3
- Familiarize yourself with the "Row, Row, Row Your Boat" activity from *I Love You Rituals*
- Watch "Step 3: I Feel" under "The Five Steps for Self-Regulation" and "Row, Row, Row Your Boat" under "Circle Time"/"Caring Connection Demonstrations" on your instructional DVD
- Watch the songs for Lesson 4.1 by selecting "Circle Time" then "Songs By Lesson" on your instructional DVD
- Gather materials
- Make foam Buddies by tracing multiples of template T.4 on foam, cutting them out and affixing Feeling Faces stickers for as many Buddies as your class requires. Purchase additional stickers at ConsciousDiscipline.com (optional)
- **Word Wall:** Merrily

Buddy Tip: Teaching your students to help (coach) the Buddies is the most important step because we are teaching them the language of self-regulation. Slow this down, take time with this step and model it often once children begin choosing their Buddies. You may choose to divide this lesson into two sessions. Stop after Row, Row, Row Your Boat. Then complete the lesson the next day.

Adaptations for Younger Students: Post a partner chart for visual support when you play partner games. Use small photos of the students. On Monday, assign "Partner of the Week" by putting the students' images next to each other in pairs on the chart. Rotate partners each week.

Conscious Discipline Tip: In the School Family, the focus is on physical, social and emotional safety. Without safety, learning cannot occur. The teacher is the Safekeeper whose job description is "to keep the classroom safe." The students' job is "to help keep the classroom safe." Everyone is united in the goal of creating a safe learning environment where all members thrive. Learn more about the Safekeeper job description and why it is vital to academic and social success in *Conscious Discipline*, Chapter 1 and *Creating the School Family*, Chapter 5.

Let's Get Started

We have learned four ways to calm ourselves when our emotions are strong. Point to the visual icons of the four calming strategies from the Step 2 sentence strip.

Calming down helps us take off the *I Am Upset Smock* and get ahold of our emotions. Today we are going to pair up and learn how to help our Feeling Buddies feel safe.

First, we are going to practice keeping one another safe by playing an I Love You Ritual called "Row, Row, Row Your Boat." Have the children find a partner for this activity. One child will be the boat and the other child will be the passenger who sits in the boat. Demonstrate this positioning for the children.

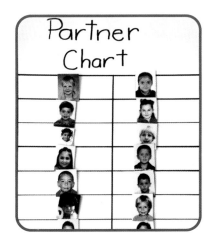

In our classroom, my job is to keep everyone safe. Your job is to help keep each other safe. If you are the boat during this song, your job is to help keep your passenger safe.

First we are going to sing with nice, sunny voices. Hold your partner's hands, gently row and sing:

Row, row, row your boat,
Gently down the stream.
Merrily, merrily, merrily, merrily,
Life is but a dream.

Now, this time a storm is coming and the boat is going to rock hard with the waves in a stormy ocean. Sing with a stormy voice and be sure to hold your passenger safely:

Row, row, row your boat,
Gently down the stream.
Merrily, merrily, merrily, merrily,
Life is but a dream.

You did it! You held your passenger safely.

Which Feeling Buddy shows how you might feel during a storm? Hold up each Feeling Buddy and say, "Is it this one?"

Which Feeling Buddy shows how you might feel when someone holds you safely? Is it this one? Repeat the process, holding up each Feeling Buddy.

Buddy Tip: Do you wish you had a Buddy for every student? Order additional Buddies by calling 1.800.842.2846 or use Template T.4 "Buddy Bodies" to make foam Buddies to use with activities for which you feel students would benefit from having their own Buddies.

Have the passengers get out of their boats and sit beside their partners. Give each set of partners a Feeling Buddy or foam Buddy. (If you have enough Feeling Buddies or foam Buddies for every child, give one to each.) Have children look at their Buddy's face and name it. Then have them hold their Buddy face down in their laps so it looks like they are holding blank-faced Buddies. Demonstrate this for the children.

We are going to learn how to help our Buddies.
You are going to repeat the words.
I will say a line and then we will repeat it.
The first feeling we are going to sing about is "angry."
If your Feeling Buddy is Angry, you can turn your Buddy over to look at Angry's face while you sing.
The rest of us will hold our Buddies face down and pretend we are holding Angry as we speak.
Ready, pick up your Buddy. Hello Angry.

Conscious Discipline Tip: Dr. Bailey's *I Love You Rituals* are simple, fun activities that increase attention span, decrease power struggles, and promote language and literacy. They use eye contact, touch, presence and a playful situation to maximize children's brain power and social-emotional potential. They are essential for classrooms with young children; however, you can use them in school, at home, between children, and between adults and children. Video examples can be found on the Conscious Discipline website.

Welcome Angry. Children echo, "Welcome Angry."
Your eyebrows look like this. Children echo, "Your eyebrows look like this." (Point to your eyebrows.)
Your eyes look like this. Children echo, "Your eyes look like this." (Point to your eyes.)
Your mouth looks like this. Children echo, "Your mouth looks like this." (Point to your mouth.)
You seem angry. You are safe. Children echo, "You are safe."
Breathe with me. Children echo, "Breathe with me." (Belly breathe as you hold your Buddy to your chest.)
You can handle this. Children echo, "You can handle this." (Hold your Buddy and gently stroke as you say these words. It is important to stroke, not pat. Patting distracts children from their feelings.)

Repeat this process for subsequent verses with Scared, then Sad, then Happy.

The last two lines of the song are "Breathe with me" and "You are safe." Act out these lines as you sing them. Coach children to breathe with their Buddies while singing, "Breathe with me." Hold and rock your Buddies while singing, "You are safe."

Step 3 in our five steps is to help our Buddies feel safe. Let's review all the steps.

Hold up one finger with one hand and the Step 1 sentence strip with the other.
Step 1, I Am Angry. Put on the angry *I Am Upset Smock*.
My insides feel like this. Shake the Feelings Bottle.
My face looks like this. Demonstrate.
My eyes look like this. Demonstrate.
My body looks like this. Demonstrate.
These are my signals to go to the Safe Place.

Hold up two fingers with one hand and the Step 2 sentence strip with the other.
Step 2, I Calm down by choosing one of our four skills.
Point to the icons for S.T.A.R., Drain, Balloon and Pretzel.

Hold up three fingers with one hand and the Step 3 sentence strip with the other.
Step 3, I Feel by picking the Feeling Buddy that matches how I feel.
Then I help the Feeling Buddy feel safe.

These sentence strips will be in the Safe Place to help you remember the steps to be a helpful problem solver and keep our classroom safe.

We are going to learn a new song. We can sing this song to our Feeling Buddies to help them feel safe. You are going to pretend the Buddy in your lap is the Buddy you are singing about in the song. This is a "call and response" song. The children listen to the first line and then sing that line back as a response. You will sing the first song to the Feeling Buddy Angry.

Sing: "Helping My Buddy" #10
This is a "call and response" song. The children listen to the first line and then sing the line back as a response. You will sing the first song to the Feeling Buddy Angry.

Adaptations for Younger Students: When singing "Helping My Buddy," coach all students to keep the Buddies face down for every verse. It may be confusing to have some students with their Angry Buddy face up while others keep their faces down.

Commitment: This week we commit to choosing a Feeling Buddy to hold safely when we feel upset. We will also breathe with our Buddies and tell them, "Breathe with me. You are safe." To make this commitment, take a deep breath with me on the count of three. 1-2-3. Breathe.

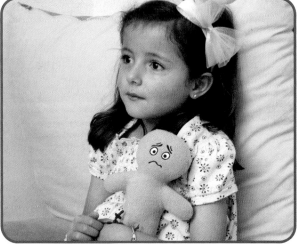

Making Friends with My Buddies

Goal: To learn how to accept our emotional states instead of pushing them away

Materials

- ☐ *Listen to Your Feelings* CD Songs:
  - "Anger Got Ahold of Me" #1
  - "Sadness Got Ahold of Me" #22
- ☐ Chart paper, markers
- ☐ Template
  - T.5 "S.T.A.R. Necklace" and "Buddy Necklaces" (optional, younger)
- ☐ Feeling Cards (optional)
- ☐ Reproducible
  - 4.2 A (optional, older)
- ☐ Instructional DVD

Word Wall

Struggle

Before You Begin

- Gather materials
- See how to safely role-play today's activity by watching the "Anger Got Ahold of Me Activity" under "Circle Time"/"Caring Connection Demonstrations" on the instructional DVD
- Watch the songs for Lesson 4.2 by selecting "Circle Time" then "Songs By Lesson" on your instructional DVD
- Make Buddy Necklaces and a S.T.A.R. Necklace by printing the Template T.5, cutting them out, laminating them, hole punching each at the top and threading yarn through the holes (optional, younger)
- **Word Wall:** Struggle

Let's Get Started

When we sing "Anger Got Ahold of Me," we are going to do something different today. We will sing the song with a partner. One of you is going to pretend to be the angry Feeling Buddy and the other is going to be the child in the song.

Adaptations for Younger Students:

You may want to skip this lesson or complete it in two days, only focusing on one feeling each day. Depending on your class dynamics, you may also wish to break into small groups to allow you to provide more individualized support as students role-play.

Buddy Tip: You might use the partner chart in Lesson 4.1 for this partner activity, then assign roles in novel ways. The class could count off ones and twos, with all the "ones" being a child and all the "twos" being the Feeling Buddy named Angry. You could also choose roles by having the partner who is the tallest, has the darkest hair, has the longest hair or has the biggest hand be the child and the other partner be Angry.

Adaptations for Younger Students: Prior to the lesson, make necklaces from Template T.5 for the children to use as visual aids. For this part of the lesson, you will need one angry necklace and one S.T.A.R. necklace for each pair of students.

Break the students up into partners and assign roles.

When the song says, "Anger got ahold of me," those of you playing the angry Feeling Buddy will get ahold of your partners.

The partner will struggle with Angry like this. We are pretending, so remember to help keep your partners safe. Demonstrate how to playfully pretend to struggle. Role-play safe ways to struggle and unsafe ways to struggle so children are clear on the expectations. If your classroom is unable to conduct this lesson safely, skip it.

 Sing: "Anger Got Ahold of Me" #1

Buddy Tip: It can be easy to get "carried away" during this activity, and some children may continue their role-play during recess, etc. Help them be successful in keeping their partners safe by using chart paper to list ways to role-play safely. Post the list visibly in the classroom and refer to it often.

Now we are going to sing the song again with the same partners, playing the same parts. This time, when the song says "Anger got ahold of me," you are going to help Angry instead of struggling. You will help Angry by saying, "Breathe with me. You seem Angry. You're safe. You can handle this."

Play the song again. After the song, discuss what happened by asking questions that are age-appropriate:

If you were pretending to be Angry, how did it feel when your partner was struggling against you?

Did you feel safe?

Did you feel scared?

How did it feel for those of you who were the child in the song?

Did you feel like Angry was a Feeling Buddy or a feeling enemy?

Was Angry helpful or hurtful to you?

Was it easy to think and sing, or was it hard to focus and finish the song?

Adaptations for Older Students: Extend the conversation. Sometimes when something bugs us, we fight with the other person instead of helping our angry Feeling Buddy first, and then solving our problem with our friend second. Demonstrate with a common situation from your classroom. For example: You are walking in line and the person behind you keeps poking you. You say, "I don't like it when you poke me. Keep your hands to yourself," but they keep on poking. The next thing you know, anger gets ahold of you. You can poke back at your friend or you can calm down and help your angry Feeling Buddy solve the problem by asking the teacher for help.

Now we are going to change roles. If you were the child last time, now you will pretend to be the sad Feeling Buddy. If you were pretending to be Angry last time, you will now be the child.

When the song says, "Sadness got ahold of me," Sad will grab ahold of you.

During the first verse, you will struggle with sadness by safely trying to push Sad away.

Remember, we are pretending, so help keep your partner safe! Refer to the chart.

In the second verse, you will help Sad. I will help you know when to struggle and when to be helpful.

Adaptations for Younger Students: Give each pair of children a Sad feeling necklace and S.T.A.R. necklace if you have chosen to use these visual aids.

 Sing: "Sadness Got Ahold of Me" #22

Discuss what happened by asking the following questions or similar ones depending on the age of the children.

If you were pretending to be Sad, how did it feel when your partner pushed you away?

Did you feel safe?

Did you feel cared for and loved?

How did it feel for those of you being the child in the song?

Did you feel like Sad was a Feeling Buddy or a feeling enemy?

Was Sad helpful or hurtful to you?

Was it easy to think and sing, or was it hard to focus and finish the song?

What did you learn today? Validate and reflect the children's responses by saying, "So you learned _____." This kind of validation helps children feel heard.

Adaptations for Older Students: Extend the conversation.

Sometimes when we feel sad, we push others away instead of helping our sad Feeling Buddy first so we can receive comfort from our friends or teacher. Demonstrate with a common situation from your classroom. For example: You are coming to school and your cat just died. You are feeling really, really sad. Your face looks like this. Demonstrate. Your body looks like this. Demonstrate. You talk in a teeny, quiet voice. Your friends see you and try to give you hugs. You can push them away and say, "Leave me alone," or you can calm down and help your sad Feeling Buddy so you can think of a way to share what you are feeling. You might say, "My cat died. I feel sad. I am going to the Safe Place."

Conscious Discipline Tip: A core principle of Conscious Discipline is "What you offer to others, you strengthen within yourself." If a child gives kindness to others, the child becomes a kinder person. When repeated over and over, this becomes a healthy life skill. As children learn to help their Buddies name and manage their feelings, they are also strengthening their ability to name and mange their own feelings.

Commitment: Our commitment is to help our Feeling Buddies instead of being hurtful to others. When we feel angry, we are going to calm down so we can solve our problems. When we feel sad, we are going to calm down and decide how to ask for comfort from our friends. Make this week's commitment by shaking hands with a friend.

Extension Activities

All Ages

"Feelings Pass It On" Game

Make picture cards with faces expressing a variety of feelings using either the Feeling Faces stickers or digital photos. Have one child pick a feeling without sharing what it is. The child quietly looks at the person next to him/her with the corresponding expression to "pass it on." That child passes the expression on to the next child and around the circle it goes until everyone has a chance to express that feeling! Play the game again with another card and another child.

How does it feel? Discuss how our feelings and reactions to others' feelings can influence how we are helpful or hurtful.

Older

Topic Sentence Literacy Practice

Use reproducible 4.2 A "Topic Sentences" to encourage students to apply their knowledge of topic sentences, and practice the S.T.A.R. and Pretzel breathing techniques. You may wish to adapt this reproducible for use with other breathing techniques.

From Hurtful Words to Helpful Words

Present children with common classroom situations and have them write the hurtful words they might say when anger (or other emotion) gets ahold of them. Then have them write helpful words they might say when they calm down and are able to engage the thinking part of their brains. For example: A child has called you a name. Anger gets ahold of you and you might say, "Shut up, stupid!" After calming down you could say, "I don't like it when you call me names. Call me Becky."

Helping My Buddies

Goal: To practice offering empathy to our Feeling Buddy and, in turn, learn self-regulatory self-talk

Materials

- ❏ *Listen to Your Feelings* CD Songs:
  - "Helping My Buddy" #10
  - "Bye, Bye Buddies" #4
- ❏ Basket of Buddies
- ❏ Reproducibles (optional)
  - 4.3 A (all ages)
  - 4.3 B, 4.3 C, 4.3 D, 4.3 E, 4.3 F (older)
- ❏ My Five Steps pocket chart and sentence strips for Steps 1 - 3
- ❏ Chart paper or sentence strips
- ❏ Active calming icons (S.T.A.R., Drain, Balloon, Pretzel)
- ❏ Feeling cards and calming cards (optional)
- ❏ Instructional DVD
- ❏ Feeling Necklaces from Unit 4, Lesson 2 (optional, younger)
- ❏ *Helping My Feeling Buddies* Book

Word Wall

Welcome

Before You Begin

- Watch the songs for Lesson 4.3 by selecting "Circle Time" then "Songs By Lesson" on your instructional DVD
- Gather materials
- Write the "Helpful Words" frame on sentence strips or chart paper
- Prepare feeling and calming cards (optional)
- Print reproducibles (optional)
- **Word Wall:** Welcome

Let's Get Started

 Sing: "Helping My Buddy" #10

Last time we talked about helping our Feeling Buddies instead of fighting with them. Today, we will practice how to help our Feeling Buddies.

In our School Family, it's my job to keep you safe and it's your job to help keep our School Family safe. You can help keep our School Family safe in many ways.

We have been learning My Five Steps which are ways to help keep our School Family and ourselves safe.
Who remembers Step 1? Show the sentence strip for Step 1. What does this mean?
Who remembers Step 2? Hold up the sentence strip for Step 2. What does this mean?
Who remembers Step 3? Hold up the sentence strip for Step 3. What does this mean?

You got it! We can all help keep our School Family safe by going to the Safe Place and taking off the *I Am Upset Smock* by calming down by using our helpful steps. Let's practice our four ways to calm down.

Hold up the icons for S.T.A.R., Drain, Balloon and Pretzel, and ask children to review each. Use this as an assessment to see who is belly breathing and who still needs more practice.

We can help our School Family stay safe by helping our Feeling Buddies feel safe. Remember when we learned how to help our Buddies, we welcomed them and helped them. The song we sang in the beginning is called "Helping My Buddy." It shows us what we can do to be helpful.

Let's check it out by talking to Angry. Hold up Angry. Angry, how can the children help you?

Angry: Oh, boy! I've been waiting a long time for the chance to tell you these helpful words to say!

First, when your face looks like mine, pick me up.
Then, I like for you to hold me and say, "Hello Angry." Repeat and demonstrate after each statement.
I like for you to welcome me and say, "Welcome Angry."
I like for you to see me and say, "Your eyebrows are like this. Your eyes are like this. Your mouth is going like this."
I like for you to call me by my name and say, "You seem angry."
I like for you to help me calm down by saying, "Breathe with me. You are safe."
I like for you to encourage me by saying, "You are safe. You can handle this."

Wow, that's a lot to remember. I guess that's why we sing "Helping My Buddy."

Which Feeling Buddy can we talk to next?
Does someone have a Feeling Buddy that matches how you are feeling right now?
Does anyone feel a little anxious, scared, sad or disappointed?

Encourage a child to share the story of how he or she feels, and select the corresponding Buddy. Then repeat the process using the exact same words we used with Angry. Now it's your turn to practice with a partner. One partner is going to play the role of a Feeling Buddy. The other partner is going to play the role of a child.

Adaptations for Younger Students: Use your Partner of the Week chart from Lesson 4.1. Depending on your students, this lesson may be more suited for use with small groups to allow you to provide more support as students role-play. You may also wish to use the Feeling Necklaces you made for Lesson 4.2 as visual aids.

Instruct the children to pair up. Begin with scared. Have the partnered children sit across from each other. The partner role-playing the scared Feeling Buddy will pretend to be scared. Coach them to show their feeling on their faces and in their bodies. Then coach the other partner to repeat after you in a call-and-response pattern, pointing to the "Helpful Words" frame you wrote on sentence strips or chart paper as you say each line.

Hello Scared. Children echo, "Hello Scared."
Welcome Scared. Children echo, "Welcome Scared."
Your eyebrows are like this. Your eyes are like this. Your mouth is going like this. Children echo, "Your eyebrows are like this. Your eyes are like this. Your mouth is going like this," and mirror their partners' faces.
You seem scared. Children echo, "You seem scared."
You are safe. Breathe with me. Children echo, "You are safe. Breathe with me." Now lead all children in being a S.T.A.R.
You are safe. You can handle this. Children repeat, "You are safe. You can handle this," and offer a comforting touch to their Feeling Buddy partners.

Practice with as many Feeling Buddies as you have time for and the children have interest in. You will want to repeat this activity many times. It gives children the opportunity to practice the language they will use for self-regulation.

 Sing: "Bye, Bye Buddies" #4

Commitment: We commit to helping our School Family by going to the Safe Place when we are upset, choosing a Feeling Buddy that matches our feeling and welcoming them. We will help others by helping our Feeling Buddies. To show you agree to this commitment, point to the Feeling Buddy pockets three times. Ready? 1-2-3!

Buddy Tip: Teaching children to help their Buddy takes repeated practice. Take 10 minutes during Morning Circle (Morning Meeting) to give children the opportunity to practice. Have a child choose a Buddy and then as a class repeat after you. Hello ____ (Sad, Scared, Angry, etc.). Welcome ____. Your eyebrows are going like this. Your eyes are going like this. Your mouth is going like this. You seem ____. You are safe. Breathe with me. You are safe. You can handle this. (Remember to teach children to stroke the Buddy, not pat the Buddy.)

Buddy Tip: Help children learn the language of helping their buddies by reading the *Helping My Feeling Buddies book*. As you read, have children take turns holding the buddy, looking at the buddy and using the language to help the buddy. Reread for practice as often as needed as children learn to coach buddies independently. Store in the Safe Place so children can access it when working the 5 steps of self-regulation.

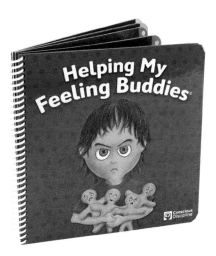

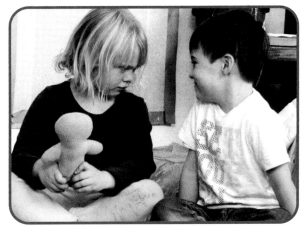

Extension Activities

All Ages

I Help Keep My School Family Safe

Make a class book called "I Help Keep My School Family Safe" using reproducible 4.3 A. Each child will name one thing he/she does to keep it safe. Older students will write their responses on the reproducible, while younger children will dictate their responses for the teacher to write. Students will then illustrate their helpful acts. You can also take pictures of each student demonstrating these helpful skills. Bind the pages together in a book for your class library.

Feelings Fun

Make two sets of cards: 1) Feeling cards each have a digital photo or Feeling Faces sticker on them 2) Calming cards each have one of the four active calming icons on them. Turn the cards over so no one can see them. Divide the class in half. One half will be "Feelers" and the other half will be "Calmers."

Choose a child from the Feelers side to pick a feeling card. The Feelers act out the feeling pictured.

The Calmers help the Feelers by repeating after you:
Something must have happened. Encourage them to repeat.
Your face looks like this. Encourage them to repeat and model their faces to match.
Your body looks like this. Encourage them to repeat and model their bodies to match.

What is one thing we can do when we feel this way? Choose a volunteer from the Calmers to come up and pick a calming card. Have everyone do that calming activity together.
You are safe. You can handle this. Encourage the Calmers to repeat.

Switch roles and repeat the process so everyone has the chance to be both a Feeler and a Calmer. Finally, conduct the activity with everyone both feeling and calming themselves with the calming language, mimicking the self-talk process they are learning.

Older

What Could You Say?

Coach students to fill in the blanks on reproducibles 4.3 B "Hello Sad," 4.3 C "Hello Angry," 4.3 D "Hello Disappointed" and 4.3 E "Hello Frustrated" using the words they learned in this lesson.

My Buddy and Me

Reproducible 4.3 F "My Buddy and Me" provides a space for students to draw a picture of themselves and write what they would tell their Buddy to help it feel safe.

Using the Feeling Buddies in the Safe Place

Goal: To learn how to pick a Feeling Buddy that matches your emotional state and how to start using the Feeling Buddies in the Safe Place

Materials

- [ ] *Listen to Your Feelings* CD Song:
  - "Yes, I Can" #29
- [ ] Feeling Buddies in their pocket home in the Safe Place
- [ ] Reproducibles
  - 4.4 A, 4.4 B, 4.4 C, 4.4 D (optional, all ages)
- [ ] My Five Steps pocket chart and sentence strips for Steps 1 - 3
- [ ] *Shubert is a S.T.A.R.*
- [ ] *I Am Upset Smock*
- [ ] Feelings Bottle
- [ ] Chart paper
- [ ] Instructional DVD

Before You Begin

- Watch the songs for Lesson 4.4 by selecting "Circle Time" then "Songs By Lesson" on your instructional DVD
- Gather materials
- Print reproducibles

Let's Get Started

 Sing: "Yes, I Can" #29

I am going to re-read a Shubert book we read earlier. Hold up the book. Does anyone remember this book? It is *Shubert is a S.T.A.R.* I will pause at different points in the book and ask you to show Shubert's feelings on your faces. We will also choose a Feeling Buddy to match Shubert's feelings.

Read the book, pausing at various points in the story to ask the children to do the following:

1. Match your face to Shubert's face.
2. Give the feeling a name by selecting the Feeling Buddy you think matches Shubert's feelings.

You did it! You matched your faces with Shubert's face and were able to pick a Feeling Buddy that had the same name as Shubert's feeling.
Which of the calming skills Shubert learned is your favorite? Who has been using them in our class and in the Safe Place?

What do you think is the most important thing Shubert learned?

Why do you think it is important to have a Safe Place in our classroom?

Let's review the three steps we have learned so far.

Hold up one finger with one hand and the Step 1 sentence strip with the other.

Step 1, I Am Angry. Put on the angry *I Am Upset Smock*.

My insides feel like this. Shake the Feelings Bottle.

My face looks like this. Demonstrate.

My eyes look like this. Demonstrate.

My body looks like this. Demonstrate.

These are my signals to go to the Safe Place.

Hold up two fingers with one hand and the Step 2 sentence strip with the other.

Step 2, I Calm down by choosing one of our four skills. Point to the icons for S.T.A.R., Drain, Balloon and Pretzel.

Adaptations for Older Students: Record and graph children's responses to which of the four calming strategies is their favorite.

Hold up three fingers with one hand and the Step 3 sentence strip with the other.

Step 3, I Feel by picking the Feeling Buddy that matches how I feel. Then I help the Feeling Buddy feel safe.

Use this chant or make up a chant with motions to go along with each step. Write your chant on chart paper and save it for future lessons.

Step 1: Hold up one finger.

Go, go, go to the Safe Place. Pantomime putting on the smock and walking to the Safe Place.

Step 2: Hold up two fingers.

Calm, calm, calm my body down. Lead students in S.T.A.R. breathing.

Step 3: Hold up three fingers.

Pick, pick, pick a Feeling Buddy. Make the sign for "pick" with the thumb and index finger on the right hand grabbing an imaginary object.

These sentence strips are on the My Five Steps pocket chart in the Safe Place. This may be hung in the Safe Place or left up on the white board. Use it to help you remember how to be helpful with your feelings. At the end of this lesson ceremoniously hang the Feeling Buddy pocket chart with the Buddies in the Safe Place.

Now that you know the three steps and how to help your Buddies, they will be in the Safe Place. You will use them to flip your feelings so you can help keep the classroom safe. Tomorrow we will practice flipping our feelings.

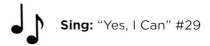 **Sing:** "Yes, I Can" #29

Commitment: We commit to changing our feelings from bug crazy mad to oozy, doozy caterpillar calm. Just like Shubert, we are going to go to the Safe Place to change our feelings from angry to calm. Commit to this with me by being a balloon. Lead the class in Ballooning.

Extension Activities

All Ages

The Three Steps
Help students review Steps 1-3 with reproducibles 4.4 A "Step 1: I Am," 4.4 B "Step 2: I Calm" and 4.4 C "Step 3: I Feel." Use the simplified reproducible 4.4 D for younger students instead of reproducible 4.4 C.

Younger

The Angry Lion Game
Students sit in a circle. Select a volunteer to stomp around the outside of the circle as the children sing, "I feel, I feel, I feel like an angry lion. I feel, I feel, I feel like an angry lion."

The stomping child picks another child to join him and they enter the center of the circle which represents the Safe Place. They face each other and S.T.A.R. three times. Then they walk together around the inside of the circle as everyone sings, "I choose, I choose, I choose to S.T.A.R. in the Safe Place. I choose, I choose, I choose to S.T.A.R. in the Safe Place." Repeat with another angry lion.

Flipping Our Feelings

Goal: To understand we can manage and change our feelings by keeping them safe

Materials

- [ ] *Listen to Your Feelings* CD
  Song:
  - "Helping My Buddy" #10
- [ ] Basket of Buddies (optional)
- [ ] Reproducible
  - 4.5 A (optional, older)
- [ ] Sentence strips for Steps 1, 2 and 3 from the My Five Steps pocket chart
- [ ] *Shubert is a S.T.A.R.*
- [ ] Tongue depressors
- [ ] Feeling Faces stickers
- [ ] *I Am Upset Smock*
- [ ] Feelings Bottle
- [ ] Active calming icons
- [ ] Instructional DVD

Before You Begin

- Watch the songs for Lesson 4.5 by selecting "Circle Time" then "Songs By Lesson" on your instructional DVD
- Gather materials
- Make a demonstration set of Feeling Flip Sticks using the instructions in the lesson text

Let's Get Started

 Sing: "Helping My Buddy" #10

 **Buddy Tip:** This lesson is more suited for a smaller group. Placing the stickers on the tongue depressors can be challenging. Working with a small group allows you to assist children. If you are unable to work in a small group preassemble the Feeling Flip Sticks following directions in the lesson. Use Happy, Sad, Angry and Calm.

Yesterday we learned Step 3, choosing a Buddy. Let's take turns practicing the three steps. We will all pretend we're doing the three steps together as we say our chant from yesterday.

Step 1: Hold up one finger.
Go, go, go to the Safe Place. Pantomime putting on the smock and walking to the Safe Place.

Step 2: Hold up two fingers.
Calm, calm, calm my body down. Lead students in S.T.A.R. breathing.

Step 3: Hold up three fingers.
Pick, pick, pick a Feeling Buddy. Make the sign for "pick" with the thumb and index finger on the right hand grabbing an imaginary object.

Today we are going to make a Feeling Flip Stick. Hold up a Flip Stick as an example. **The Flip Stick will remind you that you have the power, just like Shubert, to change your feelings from bug crazy mad to oozy, doozy caterpillar calm.**

To make your Flip Stick, I will give you a tongue depressor (hold up the tongue depressor) **and Feeling Faces stickers.** Hold up a page of Feeling Faces stickers.

Buddy Tip: This is a great Parent Night activity to help explain how you use the Safe Place as a self-regulation learning center. Parents can make Flip Sticks for or with their children, and you can use the sticks to review the skills you're learning in class.

On one side of the stick you will pick an upsetting emotion. You might pick angry, sad, scared, anxious, disappointed or frustrated.

On the other side of the stick you will pick a pleasant emotion. You can choose happy or calm.

This next part is tricky, so watch me before you do anything.
On each end of your tongue depressor, you are going to make a feeling sandwich.
You will start by putting the upsetting Feeling Face sticker down on your table. Demonstrate.
Then you will put your tongue depressor on the sticker. Demonstrate.
To finish your sandwich, you will put happy or calm on top, looking at you, and press the two stickers together with the tongue depressor between them. Demonstrate.

Go ahead and make your feeling sandwich. Review the process as needed.
Allow time for children to make their Flip Sticks or hand out the pre-made Flip Sticks (see the Buddy Tip at the beginning of the lesson).

Adaptations for Older Students or Parent Night: Make a second feeling sandwich on the other end of the tongue depressor.

We have been learning how to flip our feelings from angry to calm all year. Show the stick and flip it. And from sad to calm. Show the stick and flip it. **Here are our steps so far:**

Hold up one finger with one hand and point to the Step 1 sentence strip with the other.
Step 1, I Am Angry. Put on the angry *I Am Upset Smock.*
My insides feel like this. Shake the Feelings Bottle.
My face looks like this. Demonstrate.
My eyes look like this. Demonstrate.
My body looks like this. Demonstrate.
These are my signals to go to the Safe Place.

Hold up two fingers with one hand and point to the Step 2 sentence strip with the other.
Step 2, I Calm down by choosing one of our four skills. Point to the icons for S.T.A.R., Drain, Balloon and Pretzel.

Hold up three fingers with one hand and point to the Step 3 sentence strip with the other.
Step 3, I Feel by picking the Feeling Buddy that matches how I feel. Then I help the Feeling Buddy feel safe.

Those are the steps to flip your feelings from angry to calm. We did it!

We will end our lesson today by singing "Helping My Buddy" to practice helping our Feeling Buddies feel safe.

 Sing: "Helping My Buddy" #10

Commitment: We commit to flipping our feelings by using our Flip Sticks in the Safe Place. We can also use our Flip Sticks to help us at home. To join in this commitment, wave your Flip Stick in the air.

Extension Activities

All Ages

Play the "Flip Your Feelings" Game

Break into small groups and only use the four core emotions. Tell students to stand facing the inside of the circle. Share a common classroom scenario like someone grabbing a toy. Ask children to use their bodies and faces to demonstrate how they would feel. Then coach them through the steps using chant from Lesson 4.4.

After completing these steps, the students flip their bodies by jumping around to face outside the circle. Celebrate their success: **You did it! You flipped your feelings!** Continue with additional scenarios.

Feeling Buddy Match Up

Put all the Feeling Buddies in the center of the circle. Describe a feeling. Invite one child to choose the Feeling Buddy that would match that feeling. Have the child take the Buddy to the Safe Place. Repeat process until all Feeling Buddies are in the Safe Place.

Older

Three Steps to Turn Mad to Calm

Students use reproducible 4.5 A "Three Steps to Calm" to tell which three steps help them go from bug crazy mad to caterpillar calm.

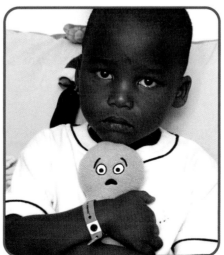

Resources

Managing Emotional Mayhem
- Chapter 3: Feeling Messages: Following Our Emotional Guidance System

Creating the School Family
- Chapter 1: The School Culture: Why traditional models are a disadvantage to our children
- Chapter 2: The School Family: Using the power of connection to create school reform

Shubert's School on ConsciousDiscipline.com/Shubert
- Click on the Safe Place to see images and video of classroom Safe Places

Shubert is a S.T.A.R.

I Love You Rituals

Songs for I Love You Rituals Vol. 1 and Vol. 2

Brain Smart Choices for Connection and Calming

I Can Calm (#B108)

When I Feel (#B111)

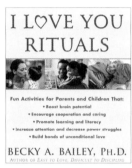

Songs for I Love You Rituals
Vol. 1 and Vol. 2

I Love You Rituals

Progress Check

Check your children's progress. Can your children:

1. Select one of the four calming strategies?

2. Choose a Feeling Buddy that matches their emotional state in the Safe Place?

3. Soothe and calm their Feeling Buddy by doing one or all of the following:

   a. Breathing with and for the Buddy
   b. Comforting and holding the Buddy
   c. Saying, "Hello _____. Welcome _____. You seem _____. You're safe. Breathe. You can handle this."

5

I Choose

Listening to Your Feelings

Goal: To learn to listen to the core messages of our feelings, motivating healthy decision making and helpful behavior

Materials

- [ ] *Listen to Your Feelings* CD
  Song:
  - "Listen to Your Feelings" #18
- [ ] Two of each of the four core Buddies (Angry, Sad, Scared and Happy)
- [ ] Templates
  - T.6 "Feeling Signals"
- [ ] Reproducible
  - 5.1 A (optional, older)
- [ ] *Managing Emotional Mayhem*
- [ ] Instructional DVD

Word Wall

Expression, Message

Before You Begin

- Review *Managing Emotional Mayhem*, Chapter 4
- Watch "Step 4: I Choose" under "The Five Steps to Self-Regulation" and the "Introduction to Caring Connections" by selecting "Circle Time" then "Caring Connections Demonstrations" on your instructional DVD
- Watch the songs for Lesson 5.1 by selecting "Circle Time" then "Songs By Lesson" on your instructional DVD
- Print reproducibles
- Gather materials
- Make your Feeling Signals poster, using Template T.6
- Write the Feeling Buddies Messages on sentence strips or chart paper (For Pre-K, K and First Grade, put the Feeling Buddy icon on the sentence strip with the message)
- Prepare your I Choose To Think poster by affixing the loop side of Velcro to the poster and the fuzz side to the choices
- **Word Wall:** Expression, Message

Let's Get Started

 Sing: "Listen to Your Feelings" #18

Today we are going to play a game called "Guess My Name" using the Feeling Signals poster. Point to the poster. **Then we are going to learn about the whisper messages of feelings.** Provide a visual to the children by pretending to whisper in someone's ear.

How exciting! I wonder what those messages could be. We will find out soon, but first let's play our game.

Buddy Tip: Emotions serve four basic functions. First, they ensure our survival. They provide warning signals that prepare us for actions like running away, avoiding someone or fighting back. Second, they motivate us to act. Our muscles tense or relax and our blood vessels dilate or constrict, providing uncomfortable sensations that send us the signal to do something. Third, they provide internal signals essential to decision making. Emotions become a moral compass to determine whether something aligns with our values. Finally, they provide social signals to others. They help others decide how to behave towards us in helpful ways and vice versa.

Adaptation for Older Students: Instead of "face signals," use the word "expressions."

Our feelings send out signals to everyone. For example, our feelings send face signals. Point to the poster. On the count of three, everyone show me your sad face. 1-2-3.

You did it! Your face went like this. Demonstrate.
Your mouth went like this. Demonstrate.
You looked like our Feeling Buddy named Sad. Show the sad Feeling Buddy.

When I call your name, pick out a Feeling Buddy. You will look at your Buddy's face carefully so no one else can see which one you picked. Then you will decide which signal you are going to give the class. Point to the Feeling Signals poster.

You can pick a face signal.
You can pick a voice signal, the way your voice might sound when you are feeling that feeling.
Or you might pick a body signal, the way your body might look.
Then you will act out the signal for the class, and we will guess which Buddy you chose.

I will pick a feeling to begin the game so you know exactly what to do. Reach into the basket of Buddies and select a Feeling Buddy. Peek at it carefully so the class cannot see the Buddy's face.

I am going to do a body signal. Point to the body signal on the Feeling Signals poster.
Here I go! This is what my body might look like when I am feeling like this Buddy. Demonstrate.

Which Buddy did I pick?

You did it! You guessed my Buddy! Play the game with as many children as you have time for and as long as the children remain engaged. Remember, children have the right to pass.

Now, let's talk about the whisper messages of feelings. Pretend to whisper into someone's ear again. Our feelings send signals to others, just like in our game. They also send signals to us. These signals are important messages! Listening to these messages helps us feel safe and loved. Let's see if our Feeling Buddies will share their whisper messages with us.

 Adaptation for Younger Students: Whisper messages are an abstract concept. Teach this concept over four days, focusing on one feeling and the corresponding whisper message each day. Begin by talking about other messages our bodies provide. When we are tired our body says, "I need rest." When we are hungry our body says, "I need to eat."

Angry: Hi everyone. My whisper message has two parts: Calm down and change.
First, you must calm down.
Then you must choose to change from being hurtful to helpful.

I have watched you do this all year long. Show me one way you calm down. Lead the students in one of the breathing activities they suggest. Oh, that's my favorite one! It feels so good!

I've also seen you change from being hurtful to helpful. You are saying, "Move, please," instead of pushing. You are saying, "May I have a turn," instead of grabbing. Use specific situations you have noticed throughout the year.

Bye bye, Angry. We will remember your message. Let's practice saying and reading Angry's message together out loud:
Calm down and change.
Say it again with me. Point to the words on the Feeling Signals poster and read them together.
Put Angry away and take out Scared.

Scared: Hi everyone. Oooh, it's scary to talk in front of the class. My whisper message is "I need help to feel safe."

You know what would help me now? Hold me close and breathe with me.
Hold Scared close and take a deep breath.
You are safe. I am right here. Take another deep breath.

Bye bye, Scared. We will remember your message. Let's practice saying and reading Scared's message together out loud:

I need help to feel safe. Say it again with me. Point to the words and read them together.

What are some ways we can help each other feel safe in our School Family?
Record answers. Put Scared away and take out Sad.

If you teach Pre-K, Kindergarten or First Grade, divide this lesson into two days. Teach the message of Sad and Happy on day two, reviewing the messages of Angry and Scared. Keep the sentence strip messages up and refer to them occasionally so they are not forgotten.

Sad (with a very sad voice): My message is "I need comfort right now." Teacher, will you hold me, rock me and rub or stroke my little back? Comfort Sad in these ways. Yes I will. You're safe. I am here with you.

Bye bye, Sad. We will remember your whisper message. Let's practice saying Sad's message together: I need comfort right now.
Say it again with me. Point to the words and read them together.

What are some ways we can comfort our friends when they feel sad? Record answers. Put Sad away and take out Happy.

Happy: Hi everyone. It's great to see each of you! My message is "You are love and so am I!"
We are all full of love!
I am going to say my message again and then we will say it together!
You are love and so am I!
One more time! This time put your hands over your heart!
You are love and so am I!

Bye bye, Happy. We will remember your message.

Now we're going to play a game called "Do you remember the message?" Select four children to wear the Buddy Necklaces you made with Template T.5 in Unit 4, Lesson 2. Have them stand in various locations around the room.

I'm going to read a message from the Feeling Messages chart. When I finish reading the message, walk safely and carefully to the Feeling Buddy face you think tells you that message. Who can demonstrate what walking safely and carefully will look like?

Select a student to demonstrate safe walking, and then begin the game. Rotate wearing the necklaces and moving so everyone has a turn.

 Sing: "Listen to Your Feelings" #18

Commitment: Our commitment this week is to start listening to our feelings. If you feel scared, you might say, "I need some help." If you feel sad, you might say, "I need some comfort." If you feel angry, you might go to the Safe Place and say, "I need to calm down and change." And if you feel happy, you might smile because you know you are loved. Raise your hand if you want to practice this week? Pause. Me too!

Extension Activities

Younger

Play "Telephone" (Small Group Activity)
Hold up a Feeling Buddy (Sad, Happy, Scared or Angry) and then whisper pass the message around the circle. After the children know the messages, pass the message and then have them pick up the Feeling Buddy that matches the message.

Older

Speech Bubbles
Use this lesson to teach speech bubbles. Speech bubbles indicate what a person or character is saying. In reproducible 5.1 A "Whisper Messages," children will match the speech bubble to the corresponding Feeling Buddy. You may also want to use this lesson to teach quotation marks.

Buddy Tip: The book *Helping My Feeling Buddies* gives children the images and language to go to the Safe Place, help their Feeling Buddies and hear the whisper message.

Turning on My Thinking Brain

Goal: To learn how to turn on your thinking brain by writing or drawing about emotional situations

Materials

- [ ] *Listen to Your Feelings* CD Song:
  - "Feeling Buddies Rap" #7
- [ ] Basket of Buddies
- [ ] My Five Steps pocket chart with sentence strips for Steps 1-4
- [ ] The chant chart paper from Unit 4, Lesson 4
- [ ] I Choose to Think poster
- [ ] *I Am Upset Smock*
- [ ] Box for your Safe Place Case
- [ ] Paper, markers, crayons
- [ ] Circuit board (optional) (older classrooms)
- [ ] Instructional DVD

Before You Begin

- Label a box "Safe Place Case"
- Add a notebook, drawing paper, pencils, markers and crayons to your Safe Place Case
- Add Step 4 to the chant chart paper from Unit 4, Lesson 4
- Watch the songs for Lesson 5.2 by selecting "Circle Time" then "Songs By Lesson" on your instructional DVD
- Make an electric circuit board (optional)
- Make sure children can see into the Safe Place from where they are seated
- Place paper, markers and pens at work stations

Buddy Tip: The fourth step in the self-regulation process is choosing to turn on your thinking brain. We can do this in a number of ways we will explore throughout this unit. The I Choose to Think poster is part of the Safe Place. As you introduce each item on the I Choose to Think poster, make sure you put the necessary tools in the Safe Place Case. This lesson involves journaling and drawing, so put these items in your case.

Let's Get Started

 Sing: "Feeling Buddies Rap" #7

Last time, we talked about the whisper messages of feelings. We sang some of these messages in the song. Who heard them in the "Feeling Buddies Rap?"
Angry said, "I'm saying make a change."
Sad said, "I am saying seek comfort."
Scared said, "Safety is what I need."
Happy said, "Help a friend and have fun."
Hold up each Feeling Buddy as you talk about it.

When we get lost in a feeling, we can't hear its whisper message. We can only listen to our feelings messages after we calm down. That is why we call them "whisper messages." We have to be relaxed and calm to hear them.

When feelings get ahold of us, our thinking brains turn off and we can do or say hurtful things. We can't hear the whisper message. Demonstrate turning your brain off by lowering your head as you have done in earlier lessons.

There are five steps for learning how to manage our emotions and solve our problems in helpful ways. Today we are going to talk about Step 4, I Choose. Show the sentence strip. **Do you remember our chant and the hand motions we did?**

 Buddy Tip: The Buddy Helper can be in charge of moving the My Five Steps pocket chart from the Safe Place to large group time and returning it.

Calm: Let me lead this chant.

Happy: Want to do it together?

Calm: Okay. Let's do it. That would be fun. Follow us and do what we do.

Step 1: Hold up one finger.
Go, go, go to the Safe Place. Pantomime putting on the smock.

Step 2: Hold up two fingers.

Calm, calm, calm my body down. Lead students in Draining.

Step 3: Hold up three fingers.

Pick, pick, pick a Feeling Buddy. Make the sign for "pick" with the thumb and index finger on the right hand grabbing an imaginary object.

Step 4: Hold up four fingers.

Turn, Turn, Turn on your thinking brain. Students start with their heads down, use their hand to pretend to turn a key by their heads, lift up their heads and point to their brains.

Angry: You did it! Let's all take a deep breath and be a S.T.A.R.

After being a S.T.A.R. I feel an itty bitty bit calmer, just enough to come up with an idea... Let's act out the steps together. Who will help me through all the steps? Select a child or use the Buddy Helper. Accompany him or her to the Safe Place to coach the steps and act as Angry's voice.

Step 1: Go to the Safe Place when your feelings get ahold of you. Have a child put on the *I Am Upset Smock*, lower his/her head and take Angry to the Safe Place. Point to this step on the My Five Steps pocket chart.

Step 2: Start calming down when you get to the Safe Place. Who remembers the four ways we can calm down? Point to the Step 2 sentence strip with the four choices. Have Angry pick one of the four choices and lead the class in calming.

Step 3: Next, pick the Feeling Buddy by the same name to help comfort.

Angry: Hey look at my twin in the Buddy Pocket. Great, you can help us both! Coach the child.

You would say to both angry Buddies,

"Hello Angry. Welcome Angry."

"Your eyebrows are going like this. Your eyes are going like this. Your mouth is going like this."

"You both seem angry."

"You are safe."

"Breathe with me."

"You can handle this."

Now hold both angry Buddies and breathe. Now, put both Buddies back in the same pocket.

(You may also keep the extra set of Buddies in a basket in or near the Safe Place. If a Buddy from the pocket is being used children can be instructed to get the second Buddy out of the basket.)

Angry: Wow! This is cozy.

Step 4: Now you are ready to make some choices to turn on your thinking brain again.

You may choose to draw a picture about what happened.

Adaptations for Younger Students: When teaching today's strategy say, "You may draw a picture about what happened, and I will add your words." We will learn about other choices later this week.

You may choose to write about what happened.
What would be best for you this time?
Show the I Choose to Think poster. The choices Velcro onto the board, so demonstrate how to remove their commitment choice.

Now we're all going to have a chance to practice this new step.
You will come up one at a time and select one of our two choices, to write or to draw. You will make your choice by gently pulling that picture off the I Choose to Think poster and holding it up.

Then you will put your choice back on the board so the next person may have a turn. If you choose writing, you will return to your desk and begin to write. If you choose drawing, you will return to your desk and draw.

Buddy Tip: Your Safe Place Case will hold all the materials children need to do the activities listed on the I Choose to Think poster. For this lesson, you will add a notebook for journaling, a clipboard with paper for drawing, pencils and markers/crayons to your case. The Safe Place Case stays in the Safe Place. (If you teach young children you may instruct them to come out of the Safe Place and get the materials to write or draw.)

Think about a time when your feelings got ahold of you.
Be thinking about whether you want to write or draw about that time.
Later, you will have an opportunity to share your work.
Call the first child up to choose. After the first child has selected, call the next and so on.

Children will write or draw about a time their feelings got ahold of them based on their I Choose to Think poster choice. Children can share their work as time permits.

 Sing: "Feeling Buddies Rap" #7

Commitment: Our commitment this week is to use the Safe Place when we need to, and to do all four steps we have learned so far. Commit to practicing the steps by holding both thumbs up and saying, "I can do it!"

Extension Activities

Older

Basic Circuitry

For those teachers familiar with the Conscious Discipline Brain State Model, this is an excellent time to teach it to your students. Build a simple electric circuit board and identify the parts with students. (Websites like sciencefairadventure.com can show you how.) When you make your circuit board, draw a diagram of the Conscious Discipline Brain Model on the board and place the light bulb in the prefrontal lobe area. When you turn on the light bulb, you are turning on the thinking part of your brain! Use the circuit to demonstrate turning your thinking brain off and on throughout this lesson.

In order to teach students about the brain model, it is helpful to attend an official Conscious Discipline workshop or view the Conscious Discipline LIVE! Set to become familiar with the material first. You may choose to teach the Conscious Discipline Brain State Model with or without the circuit board.

Cranky Cream and Calming Books

Goal: To learn additional de-stressing activities to help turn on your thinking brain, preparing yourself to return to classroom activities ready to learn

Materials

- ❏ *Listen to Your Feelings* CD Song:
  - "Feeling, Feeling, Feeling" #8
- ❏ Angry, Scared, Sad and Happy Feeling Buddies
- ❏ My Five Steps pocket chart with sentence strips for Steps 1 - 4
- ❏ *I Am Upset Smock*
- ❏ Chart paper with chant from Lesson 4.4
- ❏ Cranky Cream
- ❏ Instructional DVD
- ❏ Safe Place Case
- ❏ Several books (see the list at the end of the lesson for suggestions)
- ❏ Digital camera and book-making materials (optional, younger)
- ❏ *When I Feel* book (optional)

Word Wall

Cranky

Before You Begin

- Gather materials
- Fill a pump bottle with lotion, hand sanitizer or water and label it "Cranky Cream"
- Add the class books and Cranky Cream to your Safe Place Case
- Watch "Challenging Children" on the main menu and "Cranky Cream" under "Circle Time"/"Caring Connections Demonstrations" on your instructional DVD
- Watch the songs for Lesson 5.3 by selecting "Circle Time" then "Songs By Lesson" on your instructional DVD
- **Word Wall:** Cranky

Let's Get Started

 Sing: "Feeling, Feeling, Feeling" #8

Who heard the whisper messages in the song? What did Angry choose to do? Hold up Angry. (Answer: Be a S.T.A.R.) **What did Scared choose to do?** Hold up Scared. (Answer: Ask for help.) **What did Sad choose to do?** Hold up Sad. (Answer: Cry it out.) **What did Happy choose to do?** Hold up Happy. (Answer: Share your biggest laugh.)

Good for you! You did it. You listened to the song and heard the whisper messages. Is anyone willing to share how you have been listening to your whisper messages? Encourage a few children to share.

We have been practicing going to the Safe Place and turning our thinking brains back on so we can return to our School Family ready to learn and solve problems. We have been practicing our four steps. Review the four steps in the five-step self-regulation process with the children. You may act them out or use the chant from Lessons 4.4 and 5.2.

Notice several children who have been using the Safe Place and the self-regulation steps. For example, Madison was reading silently and CC grabbed her book.
Madison screamed, "I hate you!" Anger got ahold of her.
She immediately went to the Safe Place.
The first thing she did was Pretzel.
Then she picked up Angry and said, "Hello Angry. Welcome Angry. Your eyes are going like this. Your mouth is going like this. You seem angry. You are safe. Breathe with me."
Then she held Angry like this. Demonstrate holding Angry, rocking and gently rubbing its back.
Then she drew a picture of what happened, preparing to solve the problem with CC by saying, "I don't like it when you grab my book. Please say, "May I have a turn?"

Buddy Tip: Sometimes in the self-regulation process, children will need additional time and/or specific items to turn their thinking brain back on. You can identify these items by observing the children or through brainstorming in a class meeting. Keep these items in your Safe Place Case. Just like with adults, different children may need different things to calm down after an emotional upset.

Today we are going to learn other choices that can be helpful in Step 4. This is called Cranky Cream. Hold up a pump bottle filled with lavender-scented lotion. If laws in your area prohibit scented lotion, you could use hand sanitizer or water.

Buddy Tip: Teach the Buddy Helper how to dispense one pump of lotion to each child for Cranky Cream time.

Give each child a small amount of lotion. Teach the group how to sing and do the Cranky Cream actions as shown on the DVD. Show them how to rub the lotion into their hands, massaging with firm pressure. Then show how to pull the crankies out of their bodies by using one hand to pull the lotion off each finger on the other hand, while pretending to throw their crankies away.

Sing the following to the tune of "Good Night Ladies:"
Bye bye crankies, Pull the crankies out of your pinky.
Bye bye crankies, Pull the crankies out of your ring finger.
Bye bye crankies, Pull the crankies out of your tall finger.
It is time for you to go. Pull crankies out of your thumb and throw the crankies away.

Repeat the song several times so each finger gets a nice hand massage.

Retrieve your Safe Place Case from the Safe Place.
We have new choices in our Safe Place Case! I see the writing tools and journal from last time. And I have added the Cranky Cream we just learned how to use and some classroom books.

Show the cream and classroom books. Now show how these choices are displayed on the I Choose to Think (choose a book) and the Caring Connections (Cranky Cream) posters. Add other items to the Safe Place Case as needed for a particular class or child.

 Sing: "Feeling, Feeling, Feeling" #8

 Buddy Tip: *Songs for I Love You Rituals Volume 2* has the song "Bye Bye Crankies." After singing and moving to this song, give each child some Cranky Cream. This is a great transition or Brain Smart Start song.

 **Buddy Tip:** Introduce and teach children how to use the *When I Feel* book. Then put in the Safe Place case as a tool to help children calm and flip their feelings. The book is available at ConsciousDiscipline.com

Commitment: This week we are going to commit to playing Bye Bye Crankies with ourselves or with a friend. We will keep the Cranky Cream in the Safe Place. If you are willing to play, show me how to do the Pretzel.

Extension Activities

Younger

Safe Place Book Choices

Take pictures of students using the items in the Safe Place Case and bind them together in a "Safe Place Choices" book.

 Buddy Tip: Choose from these recommendations when selecting books for your Safe Place Case.

Pre-K and K

- *On Monday When It Rained* by Cherryl Kachenmeister
- *When Sophie Gets Angry-Really, Really Angry...* by Molly Bang
- *Sometimes I'm Bombaloo* by Rachel Vail
- *Calm Down Time* by Elizabeth Verdick
- *Leonardo the Terrible Monster* by Mo Willems
- *The Way I Feel* by Janan Cain (Safety)
- *Shubert is a S.T.A.R* by Becky A. Bailey
- *Shubert's BIG Voice* by Becky A. Bailey
- *Shubert Sees the Best* by Becky A. Bailey
- *Sophie is a S.T.A.R.* by Becky A. Bailey
- *Sophie Makes a Choice* by Becky A. Bailey
- *Sophie's Helpful Day* by Becky A. Bailey
- *Sophie Rants and Raves* by Becky A. Bailey
- *Sophie Wants a Turn* by Becky A. Bailey

First and Second Grade

- *Scaredy Squirrel* by Melanie Watt
- *How Are You Peeling Foods with Moods* by Saxton Freymann and Joost Elffers
- *It's Okay to Be Different* by Todd Parr
- *And Here's To You!* by David Elliot
- *Cool Cats, Calm Kids* by Mary Williams
- *Shubert is a S.T.A.R* by Becky A. Bailey
- *Shubert's BIG Voice* by Becky A. Bailey
- *Shubert Sees the Best* by Becky A. Bailey

Connecting with Others

Goal: To learn connecting strategies as tools for turning your thinking brain on in preparation to return to class and manage challenges differently

Materials

- ❏ *Listen to Your Feelings* CD Song:
  - • "Important Messages" #14
- ❏ Happy, Angry, Scared and Sad Feeling Buddies
- ❏ Reproducible
  - • 5.4 A (optional, all ages)
- ❏ My Five Steps pocket chart with Steps 1-4 in the pockets
- ❏ *I Am Upset Smock*
- ❏ Connecting Activity poster
- ❏ I Choose to Think poster
- ❏ Friends and Family book or board
- ❏ Safe Place Case from the Safe Place
- ❏ Shubert Puppet (optional)
- ❏ Instructional DVD

Before You Begin

- • Gather materials
- • Add new materials to your Safe Place Case as needed for your particular children
- • Watch "Story Hand," "Wonderful Woman," "Breathing Arms" and "Introduction to Caring Connections" under "Circle Time"/"Caring Connections Demonstrations" on the instructional DVD
- • Watch the songs for Lesson 5.4 by selecting "Circle Time" then "Songs By Lesson" on your instructional DVD
- • Print reproducible 5.4 A (optional)

Let's Get Started

 Sing: "Important Messages" #14

Who heard the feelings messages in this song?

Happy: Remember me? My message is "I am love." Who has done something loving and would like to share? Encourage a few children to share.

Angry: Remember me? My message is "Calm down and change." Who has done this and would like to share? Encourage a few children to share.

Scared: Remember me? My message is "I need help to feel safe." Has anyone felt anxious or scared and asked for help? Who wants to share? Encourage a few children to share.

Sad: Remember me? My message is "I need comfort right now." Has anyone given or received comfort from a friend and wants to share? Encourage a few children to share.

Let's review our steps for getting ahold of our feelings instead of our feelings getting ahold of us. I am going to tell you a story about a little bug named Shubert. Use a Shubert puppet if you have one. I want you to listen to the story and tell me what would help Shubert get ahold of his feelings.

Buddy Tip: Make up the story that has some relevance to your class and situations that are common for you. Here are common themes to spur your thinking as you choose your unique story:
Shubert misses his mom after being dropped off at school.
Shubert's friend calls him a name.
Shubert has trouble with reading or math.
Shubert has no one to play with on the playground.

An example of a story would be... Shubert was working hard to read his book.
Some of the words were really, really hard.
The more he tried to read, the harder the book became.
His face got hot. He could feel his muscles get tight.
He wanted to throw the book against the wall and scream.

What feeling do you think got ahold of Shubert? Hold up the *I Am Upset Smock*.
What would help Shubert now? Go to the Safe Place. Point to the Step 1 "I Am" sentence strip in the My Five Steps pocket chart.
When Shubert goes to the Safe Place, what could he do first that would help him? Show the four breathing icons from Step 2 in the pocket chart.
What would help him next? Pick a Feeling Buddy and help the Buddy feel safe.
What could he say to his Feeling Buddy that would help them both get ahold of their feelings? Hello Frustrated, Welcome Frustrated. Your eyebrows are going like this. Your eyes are going like this. Your mouth is going like this. You seem frustrated. You're safe. Breathe with me. You can handle this.

Now it is time for Shubert to turn his thinking brain back on so he can go finish his work. He can make a choice from Step 4 in the pocket chart or he can choose from the I Choose to Think poster.
He could write about it. He could draw a picture about it. He could choose some Cranky Cream.
He could choose a book, even if he just wants to look at the pictures.
Or he could pick one of these new choices. Point to the card that says "Friends and Family."

Sometimes remembering we have people who love us helps turn on our thinking brain. Shubert might choose to look at his Friends and Family Book or Bulletin Board.

Conscious Discipline Tip: Viewing images on the Friends and Family Board can be soothing for many children. Some children will benefit from a mini-photo album they can keep in the Safe Place with them. You can find detailed information about making a Friends and Family Book or Board in *Creating the School Family*, Chapter 4. For images and video of the Friends and Family Board visit Shubert's School at ConsciousDiscipline.com/Shubert

Or he might choose to do a connecting activity. Point to the card and poster representing the connection activities. This choice requires connecting with an adult or another friend. You will need to decide on a procedure for this within the confines of your classroom. The student could bring the card to an adult or to a friend as a way of asking for this type of interaction. Communicate your expectations and procedures clearly with words, modeling and visual aids as shown on your DVD. If you teach Pre-K or Kindergarten, first teach the children to go to an adult after selecting the connecting activity. After the children have experienced these connecting activities and become familiar with the "I Choose" step, teach children they can also ask a friend to do the connecting activity.

 Buddy Tip: You can find additional connecting activities in the *I Love You Rituals* book and under the "Resources" section of the Conscious Discipline website.

 **Adaptations for Younger Students:** Use your Partner of the Week system when pairing students. Continue to provide students with opportunities to practice connection activities with partners.

Let's practice three connecting activities. Have children pair up with each other, and teach the following activities. (These activities are on the Caring Connections poster.)

Breathing Arms:
Hold your partner's hands. Raise your arms above your heads as you breathe in. Lower your arms as you breathe out. Remember to look at your partner. Do three breathing arms. Remember to breathe together.

Story Hand: *I Love You Rituals*, page 167. Older students can be paired together. Younger students must be paired with a teacher.
We will do this one together. Hold your partner's hand, follow my instructions and echo after me. Tell your partner, "It is story time." Instead of reading a book for a story, you are going to take your partner's hand and talk about his or her day. If you teach Second Grade or younger use the example below or make it fit a student you select to demonstrate the Story Hand. Model this with one child as the class watches. You may choose to repeat with several children. At some point during the next few days do a Story Hand with each child so they can experience it. Then when they choose Story Hand to turn on their thinking brain it will be meaningful.

This is just an example. Tailor the story to your children's experiences.

Start with the pinky finger, giving it a nice massage and saying, "This little finger got up really early in the morning and yawned and stretched." Allow time for children to echo, encouraging them as needed.

Go to the next finger and give it a deep massage, saying, "This finger picked out clothes, got dressed, and ate breakfast." Allow time for children to echo.

Continue to the next finger, saying, "And this finger went to school." Allow time for children to echo. At the index finger, say, "At school this finger had fun, learned a lot, but got in a fight with his best friend." Allow time for children to echo.

Finally, massage the thumb and say excitedly, "And the thumb was a little scared maybe he had lost a good friend." Allow time for children to echo.

Then tuck the thumb into the palm of your partner's hand and wrap all the other fingers over the thumb. Say reassuringly, "Don't you worry. People who love each other sometimes have fights, but they find a way to solve the problem just like you will."

Wonderful Woman: *I Love You Rituals*, page 59 and *Songs for I Love You Rituals Volume 1.* This activity can be done two ways. One can be seen on the DVD and the other is provided below. If you do not know the tune, it can be spoken like a nursery rhyme. Make the connection even more meaningful by slowing down the activity during adult/child pairings.

"A wonderful woman lived in a shoe." Turn your partner's hands so they're facing you, palms out. Give a hand massage.
"She had so many children." Touch each finger on your partner's hand as you say each word.
"She knew exactly what to do." Touch each finger on the other hand as you say each word in this line.
"She held them." Fold your partner's fingers into fists and put your hands around them.
"She rocked them." Rock your partner's hands side to side within your own.
"And tucked them in bed." Press your partner's hands against your chest.
"I love you, I love you, is what she said." Say these words lovingly and give your partner a hug.

Bye Bye Crankies

This is the ritual you learned in the last lesson. Practice it again if you have time.

 Sing: "Important Messages" #14

Commitment: The commitment this week is for you to teach a connecting activity to a parent, sibling, grandparent or other family member. If you commit to teaching someone a connecting activity, raise your hand.

Extension Activities

All Ages

Sequencing

Using reproducible 5.4 A, students will put the four steps in the order they would do them in the Safe Place by writing the number in the box. Place a "1" in the box beside Step 1, a "2" for Step 2, etc. Younger children can cut the steps out and paste them in the correct order.

I Have Choices

Goal: To listen to the signals and whisper messages of our feelings so we can be helpful to each other and ourselves

Materials

- [ ] *Listen to Your Feelings* CD
  Song:
  - "I Have a Choice" #12
- [ ] Angry, Sad, Scared and Happy Feeling Buddies
- [ ] Reproducible
  - 5.5 A
- [ ] Feeling Buddies messages sentence strips or chart paper from Lesson 5.1
- [ ] Chart paper
- [ ] Instructional DVD

Before You Begin

- Watch the "I Have a Choice" video on the DVD
- Gather materials
- Print reproducibles
- Watch the songs for Lesson 5.1 by selecting "Circle Time" then "Songs By Lesson" on your instructional DVD

Buddy Tip: If you teach Pre-K, Kindergarten or First Grade this lesson is more effective if done in small group. Follow the lesson but only have one child stand up holding a Buddy. Display all four messages on the sentence strips and have the small group choose the message of the Buddy standing. Then follow the directions for demonstrating face, body and voice signals. Brainstorm responses for that Buddy. Then move onto the next Buddy. Slowing down and highlighting one Buddy at a time will help young children deepen their understanding of the messages and how they can help the Buddy.

Let's Get Started

 Sing: "I Have a Choice" #12

Today we are going to practice being helpful to our friends when we see their feeling signals on their face (make an angry face), **hear it in their voices** (say, "I hate you" loudly), or **see it in their bodies** (tense your body and make fists).

Display the four feeling messages and the four core Feeling Buddies: Angry, Sad, Scared and Happy. We are going to play a game called "I Can Be Helpful By _____."

Adaptations for Younger Students: Teach this lesson over multiple days. Help children focus on what to do to help themselves first, and then focus on how to help a friend.

To play the game, choose eight children to stand in front of the class. Hand out the four Feeling Buddies to four of the children. Hand out the four feeling messages to the four other children.

The goal is for the children with the feeling messages to match their message with the correct Buddy by walking over to the corresponding Buddy. Play the game until 100 percent accuracy is achieved. If children have trouble, have the Feeling Buddies talk and help them.

Conscious Discipline Tip: In Conscious Discipline, children learn how to wish each other well. Wishing well happens when we take a deep breath, put our attention to our heart (older) or hands over our heart (younger) and send out loving energy. Sometimes when we experience intense emotions, we want or need to be left alone. Teach children that during times like those, they can help their friends from a distance by wishing them well.

Next, ask the child holding the sad Feeling Buddy to demonstrate sad face, voice and body signals.
What could Sad do to get comfort? Write down the children's responses on chart paper.
What could we do to help Sad? Write down children's responses.

Ask the child holding the angry Feeling Buddy to demonstrate angry face, voice and body signals.
What could Angry do to calm down? Write children's responses.
What could we do to help Angry? Write children's responses.

Ask the child holding the scared Feeling Buddy to demonstrate scared face, voice and body signals.
What could Scared do to feel safe? Write children's responses.
What could we do to help Scared? Write children's responses.

Ask the child holding the happy Feeling Buddy to demonstrate happy face, voice and body signals.
What could Happy do to share love? Write children's responses.
What could we do to help Happy share love? Write children's responses.

Adaptations for Older Students: Complete this lesson pattern for all eight Buddies.

Now it's your turn to decide what you would do to help yourself when you are feeling Sad, Angry, Scared or Happy. Hand out reproducible 5.5 A "I Can Be Helpful" and tell children to fill in how they would choose to be helpful. Assist younger children as necessary.

 Sing: "I Have a Choice" #12

Commitment: Our commitment is to help friends when anger or frustration gets ahold of them. We will do this by being a S.T.A.R., and saying, "Breathe with me, you can handle this." Make this commitment now by practicing with me on the count of three. 1-2-3. Lead children in being a S.T.A.R. and saying, "Breathe with me, you can handle this."

Resources

Managing Emotional Mayhem
- Chapter 3: Feeling Messages: Following Our Emotional Guidance System
- Chapter 4: The Adult Journey: Five Steps for Self-Regulation
- Chapter 5: The Child's Journey: Coaching Children in the Five-Step Process

Creating the School Family
- Chapter 4: Friends and Family Board
- Chapter 9: Safe Place
- Chapter 10: School Family Rituals

Shubert's School on ConsciousDiscipline.com/Shubert
- Click the circular Wish Well Board to see video of children wishing well
- Click the Friends and Family Board to see this structure in use

I Love You Rituals

Shubert's Classroom

Shubert Puppet with
Dr. Becky Bailey

I Solve

Seeing with Loving Eyes

Goal: To help children see problems as opportunities to help themselves and their friends learn new social skills

Materials

- [ ] *Listen to Your Feelings* CD
  Song:
  - "It's Okay" #17
- [ ] Angry Feeling Buddy
- [ ] Reproducibles
  - 6.1 A (optional, younger)
  - 6.1 B (optional, older)
- [ ] Template
  - T.7 "See the Best Glasses"
- [ ] Markers, crayons, stickers, etc., to decorate the glasses
- [ ] *Shubert Sees the Best*
- [ ] *Managing Emotional Mayhem*
- [ ] Instructional DVD

Before You Begin

- Review *Managing Emotional Mayhem*, Chapter 5
- Watch "Step 5: I Solve" under "The Five Steps to Self-Regulation" on your instructional DVD
- Watch the songs for Lesson 6.1 by selecting "Circle Time" then "Songs By Lesson" on your instructional DVD
- Gather materials
- Print reproducibles
- Make a sample pair of See the Best Glasses by printing and cutting out Template T.7, gluing a tongue depressor to the side of the glasses and then decorating them.

Let's Get Started

♩♪ **Sing:** "It's Okay" #17

In this song it says, "It's okay to feel that way." We've already learned our feelings are our friends. They are our Buddies! Do you think this means we can be hurtful to others if we feel angry? What must we do with our anger to make sure we are helpful instead of hurtful?

Remember to reflect children's responses back to them. You might say, "So you think ____." Let them truly express themselves. Be careful not to judge their responses or imply they are wrong. We often do this by saying things like, "Are you sure that would be a good idea?"

When our feelings get ahold of us, sometimes we act in hurtful ways. That is why we practice getting ahold of our feelings. Once we get ahold of our feelings, we can turn our thinking brains on, see things differently and learn new ways of solving problems.

Look at this book. Hold up the book. Do you recognize this character? Who remembers his name? The name of this book is *Shubert Sees the Best*.

Conscious Discipline Tip: Our perception dictates our behavior. Perceptual changes are essential for permanent behavioral changes. Historically, we have taught children that bad behavior equals bad children and good behavior equals good children. Conscious Discipline asks us to shift away from judging children and their behavior as good or bad, instead seeing conflict and upset as a reflection of missing social-emotional skills. As we make this shift, we teach children to see conflict differently. Children no longer see each other as mean, but as needing help learning new ways to communicate. If we ever hope to end children's bullying, adults must let go of the belief that guilt, punishment and/or revenge are effective strategies for helping children learn life skills.

Adaptations for Younger Students: Prepare the glasses ahead of time. Allow students to decorate the glasses using markers, stickers, etc.

Read *Shubert Sees the Best*. As you read the book, use a pair of heart-shaped glasses to help children learn to see the situation differently. If you are already using Conscious Discipline you may have already read *Shubert Sees the Best*. Reread the book and follow the *Curriculum*. We recommend reading the Shubert books many times during the course of the school year.

Now you are each going to make your own pair of funny heart-shaped glasses. Provide the children with the See the Best Glasses template, markers and other items needed to decorate their glasses. After the children have decorated their glasses, use them in the game "Using My Loving Eyes."

To play "Using My Loving Eyes," you will use three hurtful classroom situations. You will ask the children to see the conflict in a common way (mean, on purpose, etc.) or in a more conscious, loving way (needs help to do it differently). The following examples will spark your thinking. For greatest impact, use common situations from your classroom.

Conflict 1: You are sitting on the floor.

A friend is walking past you and steps on your hand.

Without the glasses, you might think your friend is being mean, did it on purpose or doesn't like you anymore.

Now, let's put on our funny heart-shaped glasses, breathe and see through loving eyes.

Maybe your friend needs help to remember to walk slowly and safely.

We could say, "Ouch, that hurts. Please walk around me."

Say that with me. "Ouch, that hurts. Please walk around me."

Conflict 2: You are standing in line and a friend starts pushing you.

Without your glasses you might think your friend is being rude or picking on you.

Now everyone put on their funny heart-shaped glasses and breathe.

What help do you think your friend needs?

We could say, "I don't like it when you push me. Stand with your hands to yourself."

Depending on the children's responses, you will need to adjust your statement. Always start the statement with "I don't like it when you _____." End the statement with what you want the other child to do, "Please_____." We will revisit this formula in Unit 6, Lesson 3.

Conflict 3: You are holding a book. A friend walks up to you and says, "Can I see it?" You say, "No," and the friend grabs the book.

Anger gets ahold of you, your thinking brain turns off and you can't find your funny heart-shaped glasses. You might see the person as really, really mean and want to grab the book back or even hit to get it. What can you do?

You must turn your thinking brain on and find your funny heart-shaped glasses before you can solve the problem. How do you do that?

Help the children review the first four steps of the self-regulation process learned in the previous lessons.

1. Go to the Safe Place when your feelings get ahold of you.
2. Start calming down when you get to the Safe Place.
3. Name your feeling and pick the Feeling Buddy by the same name to help comfort. In this example, you would choose Angry because your friend grabbed your book. Hold up Angry. You would tell Angry, "Hello Angry. Welcome Angry. Your face is going like this. You seem angry. Breathe with me. You can handle this."
4. Now you are ready to make some choices to turn on your thinking brain again. You might choose to draw a picture about what happened.

Now that your thinking brain is turned back on, you can put on your funny heart-shaped glasses and see the situation differently. Without the glasses, you might see your friend as mean.

Now let's put the glasses on, breathe and see it through loving eyes. How could you see it differently?

You might see that your friend needs help remembering to say, "May I see the book when you are finished with it?"

To help remind your friend how to ask instead of grab, you could say, "I don't like it when you grab my things. When you want a turn say, *Can I see it when you are finished?*"

 Sing: "It's Okay" #17

 Adaptations for Younger Students: Continue to play the "Using My Loving Eyes" game throughout the day to give students more opportunities to see the best in others.

Commitment: Our commitment this week is to practice seeing through loving eyes. If you are willing to practice this together this week, put on your heart-shaped glasses. Good for you! I am going to practice also.

Extension Activities

All Ages

Shubert Sees the Best

Use the *Shubert Sees the Best* reproducible for your age group, 6.1 A (younger) or 6.1 B (older).

Younger

Book Practice

Read a common story such as *The Three Little Pigs*. Ask questions related to seeing the best in others. How could we see the big bad wolf differently? What could the wolf have wanted?

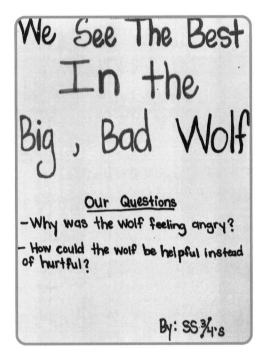

Using Your BIG Voice

Goal: Learning the skill of assertiveness; using your BIG Voice when bullied and how to ask for help

Materials

- ☐ *Listen to Your Feelings* CD
  Songs:
  - "Breathe" #2
  - "Yes, I Can" #29
- ☐ Basket of Buddies
- ☐ Reproducibles
  - 6.2 A (optional, younger)
  - 6.2 B (optional, older)
- ☐ *Shubert's BIG Voice*
- ☐ Chart paper
- ☐ Turn and Talk sticks (optional, younger)
- ☐ Instructional DVD

Before You Begin

- Watch the songs for Lesson 6.2 by selecting "Circle Time" then "Songs By Lesson" on your instructional DVD
- Gather materials
- Print reproducibles
- Write "Two helpful ways to use your BIG Voice" on chart paper

Let's Get Started

 Sing: "Breathe" #2

We are going to read a new Shubert story today. Hold up *Shubert's BIG Voice*. If you are already using Conscious Discipline you may have already read *Shubert's BIG Voice*. Reread the book and follow the *Curriculum*. We recommend reading the Shubert books several times during the course of the school year.

In this story, Shubert has a problem with a friend at school. His teacher helps him use calming strategies like we have in our Safe Place. Then she teaches him how to use his BIG Voice to talk to his friend.

Read the story. Stop at various points to have the children demonstrate Shubert's feelings with their faces and bodies, practice calming strategies and using their BIG Voices like Shubert.

Turn to a friend and tell them the part of the story you like the best.

Adaptations for Younger Students: You may wish to use one of the sharing tools discussed in "Getting Started."

Using your BIG Voice with a friend is one way to solve a problem. Write this strategy on the chart paper.

Sometimes it works, just like it helped Shubert solve his problem with Benny. Sometimes it doesn't work because the person you are having a problem with doesn't listen to your BIG Voice.

I wonder what you could do if that happens?

You could ask for help. Write this strategy on the chart paper.

Asking for help sounds easy, but can be hard. Why might asking for help be hard to do sometimes? How could you ask for help in our School Family? Record children's answers on chart paper.

You listed many things you could do to ask for help in our School Family. You can find an adult you know and say, "I need some help. My friend isn't listening to me." Say that with me for practice. Repeat the phrase with children. Write it on the chart paper.

I am so excited! We have learned two new strategies to help us find solutions to our problems.

First, Shubert taught us to use our BIG Voice to solve our problems, and Benny taught us it is helpful to listen. Remember it is your job to listen when someone is using their BIG Voice. You are helping solve problems by listening too!

Second, we learned if using a BIG Voice doesn't work, we could find an adult we know and say, "I need some help. My friend isn't listening to me."

Shubert and Benny were so helpful in the story!

 Sing: "Yes, I Can" #29

Commitment: Today we have three commitments. If you are willing to commit to using your BIG Voice, put your hands by your mouth like this and say, "I am going to use my BIG Voice to solve problems." Demonstrate by placing a hand on either side of your mouth as if to make your voice louder.

If you commit to listening to other people's BIG Voice, put your hand by your ear and say, "I am going to listen to other people's BIG Voice." Demonstrate by cupping an ear with your hand.

If you commit to asking for help when friends don't listen to your BIG Voice, raise your hand like this and say, "I am going to ask for help when others don't listen to my BIG Voice." Demonstrate by raising your hand.

Adaptations for Younger Students: Select only one commitment for them to practice.

Extension Activities

All Ages

Shubert's BIG Voice
Use the Shubert worksheet 6.2 A (younger) or 6.2 B (older) to help children practice using their BIG Voices.

You will need to teach older children the Conscious Discipline Brain State Model to complete worksheet 6.2 B. Teaching the Conscious Discipline Brain State Model accurately requires you to watch the *Conscious Discipline LIVE! Set*, use the *Becoming Brain Smart Presenter's Series* or attend an official Conscious Discipline workshop.

Problem-Solving with The Time Machine

Goal: To learn how to resolve conflict with peers using the *Conflict Resolution Time Machine*

Materials

- ☐ *Listen to Your Feelings* CD Songs:
  - "Solutions" #23
  - "Choose to Be a S.T.A.R." #5
- ☐ Feeling Buddies in pockets
- ☐ Basket of Buddies
- ☐ My Five Steps pocket chart with all the sentence strips
- ☐ S.T.A.R. icon
- ☐ *I Am Upset Smock*
- ☐ Shubert Puppet (optional)
- ☐ Instructional DVD

Before You Begin

- Watch the songs for Lesson 6.3 by selecting "Circle Time" then "Songs By Lesson" on your instructional DVD
- Gather materials
- Purchase or make a *Conflict Resolution Time Machine*

 Conscious Discipline Tip: Purchase a *Conflict Resolution Time Machine* or make one yourself, modeling it after the images at the end of this lesson. A felt-backed plastic tablecloth cut in half lengthwise makes a good surface for a homemade *Time Machine*. If you make your own, be certain your steps mimic the steps on the official *Conflict Resolution Time Machine* exactly.

Let's Get Started

 Sing: "Solutions" #23

We just sang about finding solutions. Who remembers some of the steps we take to turn our thinking brain back on? Point to the pocket chart and review your chant.

Step 1: Hold up one finger.
Go, go, go to the Safe Place. Pantomime putting on the smock.

Step 2: Hold up two fingers.
Calm, calm, calm my body down. Lead students in Ballooning.

Step 3: Hold up three fingers.
Pick, pick, pick a Feeling Buddy. Make the sign for "pick" with the thumb and index finger on the right hand grabbing an imaginary object.

Step 4: Hold up four fingers.
Turn, turn, turn on your thinking brain. Students start with their heads down, use their hand to pretend to turn a key by their heads, lift up their heads and point to their brains.

Today we are going to focus on the final step: Step 5, I Solve.

Our chant for Step 5 is going to be "Solve, solve, solve our problem."
Our motion is going to be tapping our brains with our pointer fingers and nodding our heads.
Let's practice!

Okay! Sometimes when we come out of the Safe Place, we still need to solve a problem with a friend. Today we are going to practice finding solutions by pretending to go back in time.
Make a rolling backwards motion with your arms, rotating one over the other in front of your chest.

We are going to pretend that we are all sitting in our Safe Place. Let's pretend that Shubert (if you have a Shubert puppet, hold it up) colored on your paper with a marker.
You got really angry about it!
Your face scrunched up like this,
Your fists balled up like this,
And you realized you were wearing the angry *I Am Upset Smock*.

Put the smock on a child. **Pretend you are all wearing an angry smock. What would you do next to be helpful?** Child walks to the Safe Place.

You remembered! You would go to the Safe Place. Then what?

Yes! You could choose to S.T.A.R., Drain, Balloon or Pretzel to help yourself calm down so you could flip your feelings. Everyone choose one of those strategies now to practice. Provide time for children to practice.

Remove the angry *I Am Upset Smock* from the child. **You did it! What would you do next?**

You got it! You would choose a Feeling Buddy and then help your Feeling Buddy. I'm going to hand each of you a Feeling Buddy to help feel safe. Give each child an angry, frustrated, sad, disappointed, scared or anxious Feeling Buddy.

Buddy Tip: If you do not have enough Buddies for all children, you can have them share Buddies, order additional sets of Buddies or make foam Buddies as described in Unit 4, Lesson 1.

Let's help our Feeling Buddies.
Hello _____. Welcome _____.
Your face is going like this.
You seem _____.
Breathe with me. You can handle this. Pause.
What is the next step we have learned?

Exactly! We would choose something from the I Choose to Think poster. Coach children in conducting the Breathing Arms activity with their Buddies. Then have the Buddy Helper put them away.

Guess what? Now our brains are ready to find a solution to our problem! The problem is that Shubert colored on our paper.

When we were Angry, we didn't know what to do or the words to say to solve our problem. Now that we are calm, our thinking brain is turned back on and we can solve the problem. Hold up the *Time Machine*.

This is called the *Time Machine*. We use it to pretend to go back in time (make the rolling backwards motion with your arms) to find solutions to our problems.

Select two children to help demonstrate how the *Time Machine* works. Ask one child to pretend to be Shubert and the other will pretend to be the child whose paper Shubert colored on. If you have a Shubert puppet, give it to the child pretending to be Shubert.

We are going to go back in time to help each other learn a new way to solve the problem.
Are you willing? Ask each child if they are willing. **Are the rest of you willing to learn with them?**
As you begin using the *Time Machine* with real classroom events, asking for willingness is the first step, because if both children are not willing to learn a new way to solve the problem, you don't use the *Time Machine*. If you have created a School Family, willingness is more likely.

Take the first step.

Let's all be a S.T.A.R.

Take the next step.

Put your hands on your hearts and wish each other well. This means you care enough about each other to work together to solve the problem.

Now, send out your wish well thoughts to each other like this. Demonstrate by extending your hands out from your chest and opening your arms wide.

Speak to the class: The rest of you are wishing well also.

We are almost there!

Take the next step.

On this step, we will all say, "1, 2, 3, let's do it." Repeat together.

Step onto the final footprints. Coach the child to say, "I don't like it when you draw on my paper," then ask what he or she wants Shubert to do next time instead of drawing on the paper.

If the answer is, "Stop," say, "So you want Shubert to draw on his own paper?"

Then coach the child to say, "Next time, please draw on your own paper."

Ask the child playing Shubert, "Can you do that next time?" and wait for a response.

 Conscious Discipline Tip: You have not solved the problem until you tell the other person what to do. Children often require assistance changing a negative statement, "Stop poking me," into a positive action, "Say my name when you want my attention." "Quit pushing in line" would become "Stand in your space with your hands to yourself." "Don't call me names" changes to "Call me by my name, Becky." The *Conflict Resolution Time Machine* comes with thorough instructions and examples. For more information about this problem-solving classroom tool, see Chapter 12 in *Creating the School Family* or view the *Time Machine* in Shubert's School on ConsciousDiscipline.com/Shubert.

Now step onto the globe and connect to show all is well. Coach the children to make some kind of physical connection to show there are no hard feelings (handshake, pinky hug, high five, etc.).

Speak to the class. Now you turn to a partner and connect with a handshake, pinky hug or high five.

We will keep the *Time Machine* over here next to our Safe Place. You may use it to help you find solutions to your problems. I will help you learn to use it.

What are some other problems that the *Time Machine* might be helpful for solving? Explore and problem-solve other issues using the *Time Machine* for as long as time allows and attention remains high.

 Sing: "Choose to Be a S.T.A.R." #5

Commitment: This week our commitment is to use the *Time Machine* to find solutions to problems. First, we will use the Safe Place and flip our feelings. Then we will ask our friends if they are willing to go back in time to find solutions with the *Time Machine*. Roll your hands in the "back in time" motion to make this commitment with me.

You Can Handle It

Goal: Learning to accept there are some problems we cannot solve and to understand "we can handle it"

Materials

- [ ] *Listen to Your Feelings* CD
  Song:
  - "Yes, I Can" #29
- [ ] Basket of Buddies
- [ ] Chart paper
- [ ] Paper and painting materials (optional)
- [ ] Instructional DVD

Before You Begin

- Watch the songs for Lesson 6.4 by selecting "Circle Time" then "Songs By Lesson" on your instructional DVD
- Gather materials
- Print reproducibles

Let's Get Started

 Sing: "Yes, I Can" #29

Did you know there are some problems you cannot find solutions for?

Sad: I know that! Sometimes I will just be with you for awhile. When you have lost something or someone you love, I come and go to help you get the comfort and love you need.

Sometimes I am just with you. There is no problem and no solution, just me and you getting through hard times together.

That has happened to me, Sad. I can remember when I was your age and my best friend moved away. I felt sad for a long time. Do you think using the *Time Machine* would have helped solve my problem?

There wasn't anything I could do to bring my friend back. It was a problem I couldn't fix. No one could fix it, not my dad, my mom, teachers or friends. My Feeling Buddy just stayed with me for a while, didn't you, Sad?

Sad: I remember that. You would feel sad for a while and I would stay with you. Sometimes you would play with another friend and feel happy again. Put Sad down and pick up Happy.

That's right, I would feel happy again for a while. Then a little bit later, I would see something that reminded me of my friend and I'd feel sad all over again. Pick Sad back up.

Sad: And I would come back and be with you some more. We would breathe together and you would tell me I'm safe. We did that for a while, didn't we?

Yes we did, Sad. We helped each other through that difficult time.

 Conscious Discipline Tip: When we see a friend who is feeling strong feelings, it is helpful to wish them well. Repeat the wish well tip from Lesson 5.5 now. Teach younger children to place their hands over their chests, take a deep breath in and reach their arms outward as they exhale slowly. Teach older children to take a deep breath in, picture something precious or happy, and visualize sending those calm thoughts to their classmate as they exhale. At any age, lead the class in wishing well whenever you notice a child in distress.

Have any of you ever had something like this happen?

Disappointed: Hey, what if children felt disappointed because they couldn't do something? Could they carry me during the day so I can be with them?

Sad: Yeah. If someone is missing their mom or grandpa, I could hang out with them! I could help them by reminding them of my whisper message, and they could help me by breathing and saying, "You can handle this."

I think that would be very helpful.

There are some problems we cannot solve. We have to accept them and let them be with us. What might be some other problems that we cannot solve? Write responses on chart paper. Some possibilities include divorce, death, loss of a job, you or a friend moving, rain keeping you from outdoor activities, etc.

All the stories you shared can bring up strong feelings. When you feel those feelings, remember you are safe. Say, "Breathe. I can handle this," and breathe deeply. Say that with me now. Repeat and coach children to join you.

Disappointed: That felt so nice. Will you hold me and do that again? We sure will, Disappointed.

Encourage children to discuss problems they cannot solve and practice calming with the Buddies as long as time allows.

♩♪ **Sing:** "Yes, I Can" #29

Commitment: When we have problems we cannot solve, we are going to say to ourselves, "Breathe. You're safe. You can handle this," and carry our Feeling Buddies with us until we feel better. Say, "Breathe. You can handle this," on the count of three to make this commitment. 1-2-3.

Extension Activities

All Ages

My Feelings Are a Work of Art

Create a "My Feelings Are a Work of Art" display. Give students the opportunity to express their feelings through easel painting. Older students will write a sentence about the feeling on their art, while younger students will dictate a sentence for you to write. Post the art on a bulletin board near the Safe Place.

Problem-Solving with Visual Routines

Goal: Develop personal responsibility by creating picture outlines for a routine to help solve a problem

Materials

- [ ] *Listen to Your Feelings* CD Songs:
  - "I Have a Choice" #12
  - "Solutions" #23
- [ ] Calm Feeling Buddy
- [ ] Reproducible
  - 6.5 A (all ages)
- [ ] Chart paper
- [ ] Markers and crayons
- [ ] Instructional DVD

Before You Begin

- Watch the songs for Lesson 6.5 by selecting "Circle Time" then "Songs By Lesson" on your instructional DVD
- Gather materials
- Print reproducibles

Let's Get Started

 Sing: "I Have a Choice" #12

Our final step in using the Safe Place is to solve our problem. What are some strategies we have learned that may help us?

We are learning a lot! We have learned how to:

1. Use our BIG Voice, listen to other people's BIG Voices and ask for help.
2. Use the *Time Machine*.
3. Accept our feelings, carry a Feeling Buddy with us and say, "I can handle this."

Today we are going to learn one more way to solve problems.

Sometimes I know how to solve my problem, but I forget. Last week I ran out of eggs, milk and bread, so I went to the store to buy eggs, milk and bread. While I was shopping, I kept thinking I was forgetting something, but I could not remember what it was. When I got home I had eggs and bread. What did I forget?

Exactly. The milk! Does anyone have an idea for what I could do the next time I want to remember everything I want to buy?

Some of you said writing it down would help! I could make a list so I remember. You can do the same thing to help solve some of your problems, too.

 Conscious Discipline Tip: Young children encode information in images. An environment with many visuals of expected behaviors and routines is extremely helpful. Much like adults create written to-do lists and record appointments on a calendar, picture outlines of everyday routines provide predictability and safety for children. Instead of expecting them to remember, visuals provide developmentally-appropriate tools to help them remember.

I've noticed that sometimes children in our classroom forget to leave the bathroom clean like they found it. Sometimes they leave the water in the sink running or there are paper towels on the floor. Use an example that is relevant for your classroom.

If we draw pictures like we are making a list of all the steps for washing our hands, I wonder how many steps there would be?

Let's make a picture outline together. Draw simple pictures in boxes on chart paper.

Let's pretend we are washing our hands. What is the first thing you do when you wash your hands? Demonstrate. Ask for each consecutive step.

We already have some picture outlines up in the classroom. Point to your existing routine pictures around the classroom.

Are there any problems you sometimes have at school or at home that you think a picture outline would be helpful for remembering? Record the children's suggestions. Some possibilities are remembering what to take home, remembering what to bring to school, remembering how to ask for a turn, etc.

Distribute reproducible 6.5 A, crayons and markers for children to write and draw.

Choose one of the suggestions on our list. On this paper, create your own picture outline to help you solve your problem. We will act out some of the picture outlines when everyone is done.

Adaptations for Younger Students: Instead of having individual students draw a picture outline, work with small groups of children to come up with the steps. Write out the steps and have children illustrate a picture to go with each step. Then act out the picture outlines with the entire class.

Conscious Discipline Tip: Take photographs of students completing the steps of this routine and add this visual reminder to the corresponding place in your classroom. You will want to do this for several routines. Younger students benefit from posting the lining up routine at the door, posting the washing hands routine near the sink and posting the bathroom routine in the restroom. (The CD *Brain Boogie Boosters* features a wonderful bathroom routine song called "I Gotta Go.") Older children benefit from visual routines for "what to do when you're finished with your work" and visual checklists like "how to turn in complete homework." Read more about routines in *Creating the School Family*, Chapter 6.

Act out the outlines together when children finish. Use their work as an indicator of additional visual routines that would be helpful in your classroom.

Now that we have our picture routines, we have learned all the skills on our pocket chart. Who can review all five steps for us?

Calm: I can!

All right, Calm. Go for it. Let's all help Calm by doing the chant and motions, too.

Calm: Step 1: Hold up one finger.
Go, go, go to the Safe Place. Pantomime putting on the smock.

Step 2: Hold up two fingers.
Calm, calm, calm my body down. Lead students in Draining.

Step 3: Hold up three fingers.
Pick, pick, pick a Feeling Buddy. Make the sign for "pick" with the thumb and index finger on the right hand grabbing an imaginary object.

Step 4: Hold up four fingers.

Turn, turn, turn on your thinking brain. Students start with their heads down, use their hand to pretend to turn a key by their heads, lift up their heads and point to their brains.

Step 5: Hold up five fingers.

Solve, solve, solve our problem. Students tap their brains with their pointer fingers and nod their heads.

You did it! And our choices for solving our problems are:

1. Use our BIG Voice, listen to other people's BIG Voices and ask for help.
2. Use the *Time Machine*.
3. Accept our feelings, carry a Feeling Buddy with us and say, "I can handle this."
4. Make a picture routine.

Wow! We have learned a bunch of important skills!

 **Sing:** "Solutions" #23

Commitment: We can solve many of our problems ourselves. If you commit to using picture outlines to help remember what to do and solve problems, give a friend a high five.

Step 6: Turn in your homework in the front basket by the chalkboard and put your planner on the stool.

Resources

Managing Emotional Mayhem
- Chapter 5: The Child's Journey: Coaching Children in the Five-Step Process

Creating the School Family
- Chapter 12: Time Machine
- Chapter 6: Visual Rules and Routines

Conscious Discipline: Building Resilient Classrooms
- Chapter 3: Encouragement

Shubert's School on ConsciousDiscipline.com/Shubert
- Click the yellow Time Machine on the left to see video of children using this helpful tool

Conflict Resolution Time Machine

Shubert's Picture Rule Cards

Shubert's BIG Voice

Shubert Sees the Best

I Love You Rituals

Shubert's Picture Rule Cards

Conflict Resolution Time Machine

7

Our School Family

146 Final Lesson

Final Lesson

Goal: To provide a ritual ending and review for the *Curriculum*

Materials

- ☐ *Listen to Your Feelings* CD
  Song:
  - "Listen to Your Feelings" #18
- ☐ All the Buddies
- ☐ My Five Steps pocket chart with all sentence strips

Before You Begin

- Gather materials

Let's Get Started

 Sing: "Listen to Your Feelings" #18

We have spent a lot of time with our Feeling Buddies. Have you liked having them in our classroom? Have they been helpful to you?

I wonder what our Buddies think. Angry, have you liked being part of our School Family?

Angry: Yes! Yes! I tend to be cranky, but the class helps me breathe.

Would you like to stay with our School Family?

Angry: I would love to. My cousin, Frustrated, and I could stay in the Safe Place. What do you think, kids?

Let's talk to Sad next. Sad, what do you think?

Sad: Oh, I like being part of the School Family, too. Everyone has helped so much by comforting me. I've been held, rocked, loved and coached to breathe deeply by lots of children. I've helped the children, too.

Would you like to stay with us, Sad?